LEARN THESE WINNING WAYS:

—How to turn your opponents against each other so that they will destroy themselves

—How to perfect your sales pitch to drive great trading bargains

—Ten apparently zany tactics that can make you the Bobby Fischer of the Monopoly board

—When to buy a "Get out of Jail Free" card for $80 and make it pay off

—The world's most effective way to raise instant cash—and how you can make your opponents pay off your debts for you

—How to stay at the best hotels—free of charge

—How to buy and sell what you don't own

—How to arrange partnerships that will leave you the sole survivor

—And every other legal and lethal trick of the Monopoly game

Remember, in the game of Monopoly, there are no good losers!

1000 WAYS TO WIN

Monopoly Games

JAY WALKER AND JEFF LEHMAN

A DELL BOOK

DEDICATION

*To the future of Monopoly® tournaments.
We wish the best of luck to all, and
the best of skill to our readers.*

Published by
Dell Publishing Co., Inc.
1 Dag Hammarskjold Plaza
New York, New York 10017

Dell ® TM 681510, Dell Publishing Co., Inc.
Printed in the United States of America
First printing—November 1975

ACKNOWLEDGMENTS

The authors are indebted to many people and several organizations for their assistance in the production of this book. The research done by the members of the Ivy League Real Estate Trading Game Association was indispensable, especially that done by the computer analysis committee. Many thanks also to the 114 members of the Cornell division of the Ivy League Monopoly Association for their enthusiastic support. We are grateful to the Walker Foundation for its grant which sponsored the 18 months of preliminary background work, and to the Cornell University Office of Computer Services for the donated computer time.

The Sigma Phi fraternity was very generous in providing luxurious working accommodations while we wrote. We would also like to thank our families and all our friends for their constant encouragement, especially Miss B. J. Gluckstern for her very helpful criticisms.

JAY WALKER is an undergraduate student at Cornell University's School of Industrial and Labor Relations. Originally from Yonkers, New York, Jay first learned to play Monopoly at the age of six, using a special "house rule" that he was the only player allowed to have $500 bills. Since then, he has competed successfully in several intercollegiate and national tournaments, capping his career to date with the 1974 United States Eastern Regional title. In his first World Championship bid, Jay placed second overall.

At school, Jay is the president of the Ivy League Monopoly Association, the largest collegiate organization in the United States devoted to playing Monopoly. His other activities include directing the Oliphant Distinguished Speakers Fellowship and heading the accounting department of the Cornell Concert Commission. Jay's advice on Monopoly has been quoted in hundreds of newspapers, magazines, television, and radio interviews across the country. Many experts hail Jay as the Bobby Fischer of the Monopoly world and consider him a certainty to win the 1975 World Championship crown.

JEFF LEHMAN is an undergraduate student at the Cornell University College of Arts and Sciences. Jeff is a mathematics and computer science wizard from Bethesda, Md., and coordinated the research team which developed the famous Monopoly Information & Data Analysis System (MIDAS). In his spare time, he is an accomplished gamesman and a frequent tournament competitor in chess, bridge, and table tennis.

Jeff is an internationally respected Monopoly theorist and currently directs the Ivy League Real Estate Trading Game Association, an intercollegiate network devoted to the development of more advanced tournament regulations for all real estate trading games. He was a finalist in the 1973 Eastern Regional Monopoly Championships and is currently the top seeded player on the Harvard–Yale–Princeton–Cornell collegiate circuit. His teaming with Mr. Walker has been acclaimed as the finest player-coach combination in the long history of the game.

This book is the compilation of several dozen lectures on the economic and psychological theories in Monopoly. It is the team's second book dealing with Monopoly; the first was an extensive set of advanced real estate trading game rules. In addition, the team is currently cooperating to produce the world's first sophisticated computer Monopoly player, scheduled to be completed on Student Management Services' computers by June, 1977.

TABLE OF CONTENTS

Introduction

Monopoly is a game of skill and strategy. This chapter explains the fundamentals of good play. Players using even the simplest of strategies can triple their chances of winning.

What the official rules of Monopoly leave unsaid has left a tremendous gap in understanding exactly what two or more players can and cannot do if they use some imagination. This chapter shows that, with a general understanding of the rules' many loopholes and double meanings, the informed player can do things he never before thought possible. The 14 most commonly overlooked aspects of the rules are explained.

The little tricks can make the biggest differences in Monopoly. Learn the skills that are the building blocks for dozens of others. This chapter exposes those mistakes which the expert never makes. Learn the fine points which are second nature to a champion.

4. The Crucial Houses—How Mediterranean Avenue Can Be More Valuable Than Boardwalk   39

One of the critical strategies of the game is clearly defined. If you control the housing market, you control the game. There are only 32 houses—do you know how to get to them first? Once you have them, do you know how to use them?

5. Investment Analysis for Funds and Profits   52

What is the best color group to own? How do you evaluate the "true value" of color groups? Learn how the power of every property varies, depending on the time and position of the game. Discover the correct way to analyze properties and their uses.

6. Strategy Selection, or Planning Your Plunder   65

What is a strategy? Can strategies really be used to win? Learn the criteria for expert strategy selection. The four most common Monopoly strategies.

7. Buy and Sell What You Don't Own (Yet!)   75

Using a variation on the stock market maneuver of "selling short," you can double and triple your chances of owning an unbought property. The important concept of an "option" is introduced. Learn how to make the dice work for you—not against you.

8. How To Stay at the Best Hotels—Free of Charge!   82

Buy and sell various types of "insurance" in Monopoly. The secret of using "contractual immunity" on your opponent's color group to make rents disappear. Employ a watered-down immunity—"free lands"—to conserve cash and minimize risks.

9. Pick Your Partner, Dough-C-Dough   93

The power of partnerships in Monopoly. Learn the way to combine forces and share your profits. Acquire game-winning color groups through shrewd partnership formation. The secrets of partnership formation which can guarantee you dozens of victories.

10. Trick or Trade   105

Knowing how and what to trade is a crucial part of the expert's repertoire. The game is won or lost in trades. Learn how to spot a game-winning trade and how to break up dangerous trades which your opponents may be plotting. Learn how to make other players *want* to trade with you. Understand and avoid the nine biggest trading mistakes.

11. The Balance of Power—Your Opponents Are Your Best Friends   119

The central theme of advanced Monopoly play: keep your weakest opponents alive while you concentrate your efforts on destroying your strongest opponent. Discover the ancient art of creative finger-pointing. The balance-of-power strategy explains how to use your friends to destroy your enemies.

12. The Beauty of Bankruptcy   130

Bankruptcy can be your key to success. Understand the effects of the bankruptcy rules and loopholes. Keep the poor sport from cheating you out of your victory.

13. Long-Term Property vs. Short-Term Cash   143

What to do if an opponent offers you a property as payment for a cash debt. An in-depth analysis of how to resolve one of the most difficult questions encountered in expert play.

14. Instant Cash—or Your Money Back!　146

Learn the world's most effective ways to raise cash on a
moment's notice. Understand the times when money is
hard to get. Explore the many ways to get your opponents
to pay your debts for you!

15. Apparent Insanity for Fun and Profit　159

The humorous, wacky, and often brilliant maneuvers
which are the secret weapons of the experts. Ten zany
deals that you might spring to raise cash when desperation
sets in. How to buy a "Get out of Jail Free" card for $80
and make it pay off! The Bobby Fischer tactics of the
Monopoly board.

16. "The Brooklyn Bridge Is a Bargain"　167

The aspects of psychological trading that make Monopoly
so exciting. Learn the techniques of manipulating your opponents. The experts' guidelines for "talking a trade"! With
the right sales pitch, anyone can sell the Brooklyn Bridge.

17. How to Spot, Stop and Top, a Cheater　176

Learn how to discover if your opponents are using any of
the 17 most devious cheating methods against you. Understand why even the slightest cheating can rob you of your
victory. The maneuvers a wary player should always guard
against.

Introduction

"There's a sucker born every minute," said P. T. Barnum, and he didn't know how right he would be! As a matter of fact, there are presently at least 104 million suckers in America! How can we be sure? Of the estimated 110 million Americans who have played Monopoly or seen it played, over 95% are under the impression that the game is won mostly by the luck of the dice. They're all suckers! We hope you're not one of them.

Monopoly is a game of specialized skill, requiring such talents as investment timing, psychological manipulation, and imaginative wheeling and dealing. It is also the world's leading noncarnival sucker's game. People who lose at Monopoly will always blame bad dice for their loss—never the winner's skill. You shouldn't be surprised that a skillful player can win consistently. Many games of "chance" incorporate large amounts of skill! Have you ever heard . . .

   . . . a poker king complain about "bad deals"?

   . . . a backgammon world champion curse "bad dice"?

   . . . a bridge life master remark about "bad cards"?

You can win swiftly and easily in your next game of Monopoly, while having loads of laughs, fun, and excitement. And there's no need to memorize a list of probabilities or to study specialized systems of play. All you need is a little knowledge of simple strategies and you'll win every time!

How can we make this claim? There are dozens of basic principles that you can apply to situations which occur in every Monopoly game you play. No matter how "luckily" or "unluckily" you may roll the dice, there are certain key factors which never change. Superior trading and intelligent investing are more than enough to make the dice a negligible influence on the outcome of the game. This book will not show you how to roll a seven whenever you want, but you won't need to—the dice won't matter!

This book is designed for the beginner and tournament player alike. It begins with the basic essentials which are second nature to every Monopoly expert, and it progresses through the imaginative concepts which are the stock and trade of the champion. The book is divided into two sections. The first six chapters discuss the essentials of Monopoly theory, rules, and strategy. The rest of the book covers the concepts and tactics which make the difference between a good Monopoly player and a great Monopoly player—tactics which have *never before appeared in print!* If you have ever played Monopoly and enjoyed the game, this book is for you. With every page you read, you will become a better player. As little as half an hour invested now can yield hundreds of hours of pleasure doing that which most people enjoy most about Monopoly—winning.

CHAPTER 1

The Basic Basics

Think back to the last time you played a game of Monopoly. Do you remember who won? If it wasn't you, don't worry—that's about to change. More importantly, do you remember why the winner won? The odds are good that he employed some of the basic strategies of winning Monopoly. What's basic strategy in Monopoly? We weren't sure at first, so we the authors decided to take a survey. Here are some of the more serious answers we received:

"Always remember to move clockwise around the board. Forget that and you're through!"

"Roll the dice with both hands."

"The car always wins!"

"Never spend your $500 bills."

"Always roll the dice on the board, knocking off your opponents' hotels if possible."

"Never mortgage the pretty blue ones."

A survey was obviously not the right approach, so we did some research. Although most readers will either know or recognize many of the basic principles which we have decided to include, it is a good idea to review them before going on to the more advanced concepts. By doing so, every reader will start with about the same amount of Monopoly knowledge, no matter how often or how rarely he has played the game. Here is a compact summary of the fundamental principles.

BUY EVERY PROPERTY WHICH YOU LAND ON. This first principle may come as a surprise to many players. Some have the mistaken notion that having

money is better than having property, especially cheap
property. This just isn't true. Even Mediterranean Avenue, with its measly $2 rent, can be a major influence in
the game. A smart player not only will buy every property which he lands on, but will also mortgage property
which he already owns if that is what's necessary to buy
a new property. There are several reasons why it pays to
by property:

1. Property can produce income. Okay, some rents
don't amount to much at first, but unless you buy properties in the first place, you will never get the chance to
buy the other properties to complete a color group.
Once you own a *complete* color group, you will be able
to start building houses and hotels. When you have built
houses on a property, the rents become quite profitable
and pay back the original cost of the property many
times over.

2. It can be mortgaged for half the purchase price. By
turning the title deed card face down, you may receive
from the Bank a loan of one-half the price you paid for
the property (the exact mortgage value is printed on the
back of the card). Therefore, whenever you buy a property, its real cost to you is only half its purchase price.
Remember, however, that you may never collect rents
or build houses on a mortgaged property.

3. It can be traded. Property is the most important
single item that can be offered in a trade. Since other
players want properties to complete their own color
groups, the trading value of a property is always a good
bit higher than the price you pay for it. Because of this
trading value, property is a good long-term investment.
In the words of the great American humorist Will Rog-
ers, "Property is a great investment because God ain't
making any more of it."

*4. It can stop your opponents from completing their
own color groups.* The more properties from different
color groups that you own, the harder it is for your opponents to trade and form complete color groups which
will hurt you. This is good defensive strategy. It has
happened that one player owned all of one color group

and at least one property in every other color group. He refused to trade, knowing that without his property his opponents could never complete a color group. He than built houses on his own color group to guarantee victory for himself. Every time you buy a property, you know that your opponents will not be able to complete that specific color group without trading with you. When you own a property that another player needs, its trading value skyrockets.

STRIVE TO OWN A COMPLETE COLOR GROUP. Once you own all the properties of a color group, you can start building houses on those properties and making it very expensive for your opponents to land there. This is the way to win. Nobody ever won a Monopoly game by collecting $22 rent on Atlantic Avenue, or even $50 rent on Boardwalk. All of a winner's efforts are built around the need to possess a complete color group, which he can use to bankrupt his opponents. By bankrupting them, he gets their properties to use as he wishes. Combining his original properties with all of the new properties he acquires from his bankrupt opponent, he proceeds to wipe out all of his remaining opponents. There are very few substitutes for owning your own complete color group.

WHEN YOU HAVE SECURED A COMPLETE COLOR GROUP, BUILD THREE HOUSES ON EACH PROPERTY AS RAPIDLY AS POSSIBLE. Examine the chart of sample rents shown here, paying close attention to the way the rents change as more houses are built. Notice that the rent due jumps tremendously when the third house is added. For some properties, the rent can increase to as much as 300% of the two-house rent.

	New York Avenue	Kentucky Avenue	North Carolina Avenue
1 House	$ 80	$ 90	$ 130
2 Houses	220	250	390
3 Houses	600	700	900
4 Houses	800	875	1100
Hotel	1000	1050	1275

This level of three houses on each property in a color group is known as the *critical level* of color group improvement. Notice also that to reach this critical level on a three-property color group, you must actually buy nine houses—three for each property. Only six houses are required to reach the critical level on the Purple and Dark Blue groups, as these color groups consist of only two properties each.

The strategy of building quickly to the critical level is probably the most widely known and seldom stated principle among winning players. It is especially important to reach this level if you are fortunate enough to be the first to own a color group. To delay building houses may be to pass up an opportunity to prevent your opponents from ever having enough money to develop their own color groups when they acquire them. Strike first and strike hard—this is elementary strategy at its best.

Of course, there are times when you can't afford to build to the critical level immediately. In such cases, build two houses on each property for the time being. A little later, you can nonchalantly buy the critical third houses. In other words:

> *Building one house . . . no go.*
> *Building two houses . . . for show.*
> *Building three houses . . . for dough!*

TRADE—THE EARLIER THE BETTER. Trading is the key to almost every Monopoly victory. Since it is uncommon to land on all the properties of a color group before any other player, skillful trading is necessary for any player who wants to win. In addition, it is important to trade as early as possible. By trading early, you can get a headstart in building houses on your color group —an advantage which your opponents will find difficult to overcome.

When trading, remember to strive to own a complete color group, not just a bunch of properties which give you a stronger trading position. Also keep in mind that the properties you trade away may come back to haunt you. Give up as few properties as possible, remembering that your opponents will trade properties which they can't use to complete their own color groups. You can always raise more money, but once properties are traded away, they are gone for a long time—maybe even for the rest of the game!

KNOW HOW THE JAIL SQUARE AND THE CHANCE AND COMMUNITY CHEST CARDS ALTER THE BASIC STRUCTURE OF THE GAME BY INFLUENCING THE LANDING PROBABILITIES OF EACH PROPERTY ON THE BOARD.

THE JAIL SQUARE

Over 150 million Americans have been to Jail, and most of them are repeaters. This statistic is even grimmer when you realize that many of these criminals are only seven and eight years old. We're referring to the Jail square in Monopoly, of course. But just as prisons in the real world have a significant effect on people's lives, so the Jail square in Monopoly has a significant effect on the entire game.

A player can go to Jail in one of three ways: by rolling doubles three times in a row, by landing on the Go to Jail square, or by drawing a Chance or Community Chest card which sends him to Jail. Because there are more ways to go to Jail than there are to do anything else, Jail is the single square landed on most frequently (or should we say "landed in"?). During an average game, each player will be sent to Jail five to ten times. There are two simple strategies pertinent to this fact:

1. When you go to Jail, you must decide whether to

pay the $50 fine and leave Jail right away or to sit back
and enjoy prison life for a while. You may spend up to
three turns in Jail, during which time if you roll doubles,
you get out free; on the third turn, however, you must
move what the dice show. Generally, while there are still
important properties which are owned, it is a good idea
to leave Jail immediately. However, if an "enemy" color
group is developed (has houses or hotels built on it),
then leaving Jail would expose you to expensive rents, so
it is a good idea to stay put for as long as you can. Another player might land on one of your properties and
give you the money you need to pay a few rents. There's
no reason to rush out of your comfortable cell if nothing
awaits you but trouble. If rents are high, serve the long-
est sentence you can (it's no disgrace in Monopoly).

2. The Jail square influences the frequency with
which players land on the other squares of the board.
Because Jail is so popular, the squares which lie six,
seven, and eight squares after it have significantly higher
landing frequencies than most other spaces on the
board. (The numbers six, seven, and eight are the most
frequently rolled numbers with dice. In fact, they constitute more than 44% of all numbers rolled.) If you
glance at a Monopoly board, you will immediately see
that the Orange group lies six, eight, and nine squares
beyond Jail. (The numbers six, eight, and nine are
rolled almost 39% of the time.) Since Jail is visited so
often, and the Orange properties are such a strategic dis-
tance away, it would seem logical to suppose that the
Orange group would be landed on a great deal. Computer testing has shown that the Orange group is indeed the
most frequently visited color group (though not neces-
sarily the most profitable).

The Go to Jail square also affects how often the different properties are landed on. Since this square sends
players away from the last street on the board, any
properties in that area will often be deprived of customers. The two color groups on that street are the Greens
and the Dark Blues. If you examine the table of probabilities in Appendix A, you will see that these two color

groups have the slightly lower landing frequencies which you would expect. Since these color groups are landed on less often, their true values are reduced. Exactly how much they are reduced will be discussed later.

THE CHANCE AND COMMUNITY CHEST CARDS

The Chance and Community Chest cards also have an impact on the play of the game. It is completely unnecessary (and probably foolish) to attempt to memorize the exact landing probabilities for each property. Rather, you should understand what makes those probabilities vary from property to property. The Jail square is one factor, the cards are another. If you read through the Chance cards, you will find that 10 out of the 16 cards in the deck send the player who draws them to another square (such as "Advance to Boardwalk" and "Advance to Illinois Avenue"). These cards reduce the probability of landing on those squares which lie six, seven, and eight spaces after Chance squares, and increase the chances of landing on Boardwalk, Illinois Avenue, and the other properties to which the Chance cards can send a player. A smart player knows that the cards influence the game in this important way, and he uses that knowledge when he makes trades.

TAKE ADVANTAGE OF YOUR OPPONENT'S MISTAKES. If your opponent seems ignorant of these basic principles of strategy, it is to your great advantage. There is no reason to make trouble for yourself by educating him. Let him learn the superiority of your play the hard way. If he doesn't know enough to buy every property he lands on, compliment his shrewd judgment! Admire the way he avoids wasting his money on "worthless" properties! After all, if you already own a property in a color group, there's no reason for him to buy another property in that color group—he could never acquire the entire color group! (If you can't say this with a straight face, don't try.)

Remember, if you fail to take full advantage of your opponent's errors, it is *you* who are making an error.

* * *

These are the basics. If you understand them, then you are ready to move on to the knowledge which will form the groundwork for all future advanced winning strategies. The first step in this process is a comprehensive review of the rules to make sure that you aren't making mistakes which can cost you in the future. Ignorance is your worst enemy.

CHAPTER 1 SUMMARY

I. Buy every property you land on.
II. Strive to own a complete color group.
III. Trade—the earlier the better.
IV. Jail and the Chance cards affect probabilities and strategies.
V. Take advantage of your opponent's mistakes.

CHAPTER 2

The Laws of the Land in the Palm of Your Hand

No matter what your reasons for reading this book may be, before going any further you will have to be certain that you have a firm grasp of what you are dealing with. A Monopoly game is a separate world in itself. It is not governed by the U.S. Anti-trust Laws, and its income tax never exceeds 10%. This entire world is governed by the official Parker Brothers rules. These rules are "the law of the land" and, like any laws, they should be understood and obeyed. If your Monopoly set is one of the older ones, don't panic. The "laws" have changed very little in 40 years. And even if you've lost or thrown out the rules which came with your Monopoly set, the rules are explained in this book.

In the Monopoly world, it's the law-abiding citizen who prospers. To be a good player, you will have to learn the rules of the game fairly well. You don't have to memorize them; you only have to understand their implications and see how they can shape strategies to overpower your opponents.

There are two reasons why it is necessary to be so conscious of the rules. First, the rules support several little-known, but legal traps and maneuvers which are by themselves enough to win many games for you, or—if you don't know them—for your opponents. Second, and more importantly, there are large "gray areas" in the rules which leave much to the discretion of the players in each game. These areas have given rise to simple, logical concepts like immunity, revenue sharing, options on unbought properties, agreements of forebearance, and priority of hotel breakdown. All of these strategies can be game-winning devices when they are employed by players who understand that imagination makes winning easy. A player can learn as many or as few of these concepts as he likes, and each can be learned without the others. Naturally, the more you know, the easier winning will be, and this book will make you an expert at every one of them.

We assume that you know how to play Monopoly, but we don't expect you to know all the finer rules of the game. After all, most people learn to play by watching others or by having the game explained to them by a friend or relative.

To explain the basic rules as painlessly as possible is no easy trick. Reading a list of rules is enough to put anyone to sleep, so instead, this chapter explains only the most commonly overlooked aspects of the rules of the game. The chances are very good that you have at some time or another misunderstood or violated one or more of these regulations. But rest assured, once you have read this chapter, no one will ever again exploit your ignorance of a rule.

1. The Bank can never "go broke." It issues "play money" if it runs out of its original supply.

2. A player gets $200 every time he passes over or lands on Go. Some players think that if they *land* on Go, they get $200 for landing, and another $200 when they leave Go. But they are *wrong*.

3. A property is mortgaged when a player turns the title deed card face down and collects the mortgage value printed on the back from the Bank. Once a property is mortgaged:

a. If it is part of a color group, no houses or hotels may stand on *any* property in that color group. In other words, you may never mortgage a property in a "developed" color group.

b. The rent remains unchanged on an unmortgaged property which is part of a group which contains mortgaged property. This applies to Railroads and utilities, as well as to properties in color groups. For example, suppose that a player owns all four Railroads, but has mortgaged the Pennsylvania and Short Line. As long as his opponent lands on an *unmortgaged* Railroad, the player collects rent on all four. (If the opponent lands on a *mortgaged* Railroad, the owner doesn't get a penny!)

4. Properties may *never* be sold back to the Bank. Money may be borrowed from the Bank through mortgaging, but a mortgaged property always remains in the custody of the owner—not the Bank—and may not be claimed or unmortgaged by any other player.

Whenever a player unmortgages a property, a fee of 10% of the mortgage value is paid in addition to the mortgage value itself. Many players agree to ignore this extra 10% fee, since it generally amounts to little more than a nuisance. If at any time all the players in your game agree to ignore such an official rule, it should be made clear before the game begins that a "house rule" is in effect and that the official rule has been suspended.

5. This next "point of law" is probably one of the least known Monopoly rules, but many players use it or abuse it in one form or another. Simply stated, the owner of a property may not collect any rent owed to him if he fails to ask for that rent before the *second person following* the person who landed on his property, throws the dice. Still unclear? Maybe an example will help to clarify things.

In order of their turns, the four players are Maxine, Mike, Clay, and Mr. Expert. Maxine has just rolled a seven and landed on Mike's hotel on Illinois Avenue. She says nothing. Mike doesn't notice that she has landed on his hotel and rolls the dice for his turn.

MIKE: Let's see, I got a nine. That's . . . What are you laughing about, Maxine?

MAXINE: Ha ha. Boy, did you ever make a mistake! You were so busy talking to Clay that you failed to ask for your rent when I landed on your Illinois

Avenue. That's $1100 I would have had to pay you!

MIKE: Well, you're still on my property. I'll collect my rent now!

MAXINE: You can't! You're the player following me and you've already rolled the dice. The rules say that if you don't ask before the next player rolls the dice, you can't collect your rent.

MR. EXPERT: I'm afraid the joke's on you, Maxine. You should have read the rules more carefully. The rules say that a player may not collect his rent if he fails to ask before the *second* player following rolls the dice. Mike is only the *first* player following you. Clay is the second player following, and he hasn't rolled the dice yet!

MIKE: That's great! Give me my money, Maxine.

MAXINE: Boy, it sure pays to know the rules!

6. If a player rolls three sets of doubles, he does not move his man the number of spaces shown by the third roll; rather, he goes straight to Jail. For example, if on your third consecutive roll of doubles you would land on your opponent's property with a hotel on it, you don't pay any rent—you move straight to Jail.

7. A player in Jail retains all of his rights. He may buy and sell properties, build houses, and in general do just about anything that a law-abiding player may do. Many players make the mistake of thinking that a player in Jail cannot collect rents. This is not so. The rules specifically state that a player may collect rents while in Jail.

8. A player may get out of Jail in either of two ways: by throwing doubles or by paying a $50 fine *before* he throws the dice. A player who throws doubles does not get to roll again if those doubles got him out of Jail. Except for the time he rolls three consecutive doubles, this is the only other time that a player does not roll again when he throws doubles.

9. The rule of "even building" seems to cause a lot of confusion, especially among younger players. It says that the number of houses on any property of a color

group may not differ by more than one from the number of houses on any other property in that color group. The only real complication of this rule is that when computing the difference in houses between two properties, a hotel is considered to be the equivalent of five houses. Consider the following situation:

JEANETTE: I think I'll build a hotel on New York Avenue. That's $500 for one hotel, right?

ARTHUR: You can't build a hotel on New York Avenue yet.

JEANETTE: And why not? I followed the instructions. The card says that a hotel costs $100 plus four houses. That totals $500.

ARTHUR: But the rules say that you have to build *evenly*. You haven't put any houses up on either of the other two Orange properties. You'd have to build four houses on each of them before you could build a hotel on any one.

JEANETTE: I'm allowed to have a one-house difference between properties. Can I build one house on St. James Place, two houses on Tennessee Avenue, and three houses on New York Avenue?

ARTHUR: Always trying to change the rules! That would be illegal, since the difference between the number of houses on St. James Place and New York Avenue would be two houses. The maximum difference within any color group must be one house.

10. According to the rules, a player may build houses or hotels at any time he desires. It is implied, however, that there is some restriction as to what may be considered "any time." For instance, it would certainly be illegal to build a house between the time your opponent rolls the dice and the time he actually moves the number of spaces shown on the dice. If this were not illegal, a player would hold off on buying houses from the Bank until he was certain that the number on the dice would put his opponent on his color group.

The interpretation which is generally accepted is that

a player may build before or after any player's turn, but may not build while any turn is in progress. Therefore, it should be a player's right to ask another player to "hold the dice" whenever he wants to build houses, but once that player rolls the dice, all players must wait until he has completed his turn before building. All players should agree to be courteous and to "hold the dice" when any player requests it.

11. This rule is rarely violated, but it is missed on occasion, and then it can have disastrous effects. The rule states that once you have built a hotel on a property, you may build no more houses or hotels on that property. Building three hotels or seven houses on one property in a color group is just as illegal as building a hotel on a Railroad or three houses on a utility. Every now and then, someone tries to sneak a second hotel onto Boardwalk. Don't let him! Boardwalk is expensive enough with one hotel!

12. There are only 32 houses and 12 hotels to be used for building. No more buildings may be added if the Bank runs out. If the Bank exhausts its supply of houses, or if players want more houses than the Bank has to sell, then a "housing shortage" exists. During a housing shortage, the Bank auctions off all of the available houses one by one. Look at the following example:

ZACHARY: I'm going to buy those last four houses.

WENDY: What do you mean by "last houses"?

ZACHARY: After I buy those houses, the Bank won't have any left.

WENDY: Oh, that's no problem. My brother has lots of Monopoly sets. I'll get a handful of houses from one of his.

ZACHARY: No, you can't do that! The rules say that you are allowed to have only 32 houses in a game. If there are any more or less in the set, you should either make up the difference or save the extra houses in case some get lost.

WENDY: I see. Only 32 houses are allowed. Suppose I

wanted to buy the last four houses too. Then what would we do?

ZACHARY: Then the Bank would auction the houses off one by one, selling each house to the highest bidder. Do you want to buy those houses too?

WENDY: I don't have to. Count the houses that we've already got on the board, and you'll see that we've already used up 32 houses. That means that those four houses are extra and you can't buy them.

13. Another rule concerning building is extremely important and should not be overlooked. All houses are bought for the price stated on the title deed card, but if the owner chooses to sell those houses back to the Bank, they must be sold for *half the price paid for them.* If a player buys a house on Boardwalk for $200, and during the next turn decides to sell that same house back to the Bank, he gets only $100. Hotels may be sold all at once for half price, or they may be sold house by house (one hotel = five houses), with each house being sold for half price. A large part of the strategy of the game concerns determining when to build, and the pitfalls of being forced to sell houses for only 50% of their purchase price.

14. No color groups may ever change owners, whether by sale, trade, or bankruptcy, while houses or hotels remain built on them. All improvements must first be sold back to the Bank before any type of transfer may take place. For example, suppose Lenny owns the Orange group with hotels on each property, and Immy owns the Green group with two houses on each property. If Lenny wants to trade his Orange group for Immy's Green group, he will have to sell all of his hotels back to the Bank for half price, and Immy will have to do the same with her houses. If Lenny were to bankrupt Immy, he would get her Green properties, but the houses would have to be sold back to the Bank first. No color group may ever change hands if buildings remain standing.

* * *

Now that we have reviewed the rules which are most commonly overlooked, we come to a more general question: how can you be sure that everything you do is legal? The easiest way to be a law-abiding citizen is to make sure that any arrangements you make do not violate any of the official Monopoly rules. Now that you know the important ones, you should have no trouble doing that. But what do you do when the rules say nothing at all about what you are trying to do? The way to be sure that you are well within the limits of the rules is to be sure that all of your agreements (a) are agreements to exercise rights given to all players in the official rules, and (b) are agreements which in no way restrict a player's ability to exercise those rights given in the rules.

A simple example of such a legal agreement is that of trading one property to another player in exchange for a second property. Many players think that rules about trades appear in the official Parker Brothers rules. Surprise! Nowhere do the rules say that it is legal for two players to trade properties. But more importantly, the rules certainly do not prohibit trading. Many who play Monopoly trade properties—that's most of the fun in the game! But how can you be sure that a trade is really an agreement to exercise rights that are legally given to each player?

If you want, you can view a simple trade as a contractual agreement between two players. If Linda and Betsy want to trade Mediterranean Avenue and Oriental Avenue, you could say that Linda agrees to pay Betsy the same price for Oriental Avenue that Betsy pays Linda for Mediterranean Avenue. This trade is really a simple agreement to connect two sales, and the rules clearly give all players the right to sell their properties.

How could a trade violate the rules? Suppose Amy sold Boardwalk to Toby with the agreement that he would never roll again whenever he got doubles. This would be an illegal trade because it directly violates a rule (a player must roll again when he rolls doubles, except when he rolls three consecutive doubles or uses doubles to get out of Jail). Or suppose Amy sold

Boardwalk to Toby with the agreement that he would never build houses on the Dark Blue group. This would be an illegal trade because it would restrict Toby's right to build houses whenever he wanted, a right clearly specified in the rules.

All of the strategies presented in this book will be accompanied by a brief description of the ways in which the rules sustain them. Realize, however, that once you begin to do more than just sell property, the game of Monopoly will be a lot more exciting and a little more complicated. Make all trades which use the devices in this book with the utmost care, being sure not to contradict any rules. If you are careful, you will be able to enjoy the full benefits and satisfaction which imaginative trading can bring.

Congratulations. You are no longer easy prey for a player who *knows* the Monopoly rules. You might not be able to quote them off the top of your head, and you are probably still unclear as to all of their implications, but you now know the important rules and you have seen the way they can influence the game. Each chapter will repeat the relevant rules as they are used and will give as detailed an explanation as is necessary for you to fully understand all of the advanced concepts. For now, you have been introduced to many of the tools of an expert Monopoly player. It won't be long before you will be able to wield those tools effectively and qualify for the distinction of being a true Monopoly expert.

CHAPTER 2 SUMMARY

I. The Bank can never "go broke."
II. A player who lands on Go collects only $200.
III. Mortgage rules.
IV. "House rules."
V. Failing to ask for rent—two following players, not one.

CHAPTER 3

Secret Skills That Look Lucky

A Monopoly game can be a lot like golf. You can play well for several hours, then make one little mistake and lose it all. Any golfer knows that it's the little things which separate a real pro from a good amateur. The professional manages to avoid making those critical little mistakes. The same thing distinguishes the Monopoly expert from the Monopoly novice.

We used to play with a friend who wasn't a very good Monopoly player. Sure, he knew the basics and some of the advanced concepts, but he just couldn't win in a serious game. One Saturday night, five of us (including this friend) sat down to a game. Since the rest of us were all college tournament Monopoly players, we decided that we'd give our amateur friend a handicap. We could have given him more cash or some properties at the start of the game, but someone came up with a better idea. Why not give our friend (call him Andy Amateur) an advantage which would be only as good as he could make it? We decided to give Andy the right to require any player (including Andy himself) to roll the dice again if Andy didn't like the number that was rolled originally. He could do this up to three times in the game.

At first, Andy was not overly pleased with the handicap. He wanted to know how his slight influence over the number on the dice for only three turns out of an entire game could amount to much of anything. Nevertheless, he accepted the offer, and play began. It wasn't long before Andy emerged as the victor, the first and only time that he ever beat us. What happened?

Andy used his three turns wisely. He waited until he

and several other players owned complete color groups. Then, all at once, Andy invested every last penny in his Yellow group. Soon, a poor guy named Marshall came around the board. He was sitting on Kentucky Avenue (which is five, six, and eight spaces before the Yellow group). He rolled a nine.

"Whew!" he exclaimed. "I missed those Yellows. It's a good thing too. I couldn't have afforded those rents!"

"Roll again," said Andy, and Marshall did. This time he wasn't so lucky. He rolled an eight and went bankrupt on Marvin Gardens. So Andy disposed of Marshall.

The next time Andy used one of his privileges was with Florence. She owned Boardwalk and Park Place with hotels, and Andy landed on Chance. He drew the "Advance to Boardwalk" card, and Florence was all smiles. Andy decided it would be a good idea to roll again, and he missed the deadly Chance square.

The final time Andy used his "small advantage" was when one of us (we're too proud to tell you which one) landed on Florence's Boardwalk. He couldn't come close to raising the $2000 rent and appealed to Andy for help. "Andy, be a pal. Please make me roll the dice again."

"Sure," said Andy. "As long as you give me that Red property that I've needed for a while."

"You're a thief, but I need that chance to miss Florence's Boardwalk. Here's the Red property—you now own all three of them!"

So Andy used up his third "Roll again!" privilege, and sure enough, the unluckier of the authors managed to miss Boardwalk. Unfortunately, we both went bankrupt five minutes later on Andy's well-developed Red group, which "Mr. X" was forced to help Andy complete.

We, the other players, were fools for offering Andy such a tremendous advantage. Monopoly is a delicate balance, and even a slight alteration of the probabilities can give one player an insurmountable lead over his opponents. Similarly, a single missed opportunity can ruin a player's chances for winning. A good player pays close attention to all the little things which can make the difference in the outcome of a game.

Here are some tips on how to make the little things work for you. Some of them are obvious, while some are rather subtle. One of the fastest ways to improve your chances of winning 100% of the time is to stop making the little mistakes explained here.

Always be aware of which token belongs to which player, where your own token is, and where your opponents' tokens are. If you always pay close attention to the game, this is natural. In the chapters ahead, the importance of position and its relationship to timing and building will be explained. Knowing where the pieces are will also help you keep your opponents from miscounting the number of spaces they move and accidentally missing your hotels.

Always know which properties have yet to be bought from the Bank. Only a careless player exclaims, "You mean the property that I landed on two turns ago was still unowned! I was so sure that you owned it that I even paid you $20 rent!"

Keep an eye on how much cash and which properties your different opponents own. An exact knowledge of who has which properties is often essential. Sometimes an opponent will think he owns a property when in fact he doesn't. This illusion can be so strong that the opponent might even try to build houses on a color group which is not completely his! This actually happened in the Eastern Regional Championships in 1973.

In the same way, watch out for an opponent who has two properties of one color group and mortgages one of them. This little trick can make it appear to the casual player that he owns only one property of that color group. Remember, the title deed card of a mortgaged property is always turned face down, and the color of that property is hidden. It is always a smart play to keep track of which properties your opponents have mortgaged. The chance that you will make a mistake which can benefit your opponent should always be minimized.

Whenever you pay or collect money, always check that the correct amount is being transferred. Often, mistakes of hundreds of dollars will go unnoticed. These mistakes can rarely be corrected unless they are discovered right away. Don't let yourself pay for three houses when only two are put on your properties. There are plenty of useful places to put your money—don't throw it down the drain. On the other side of the coin, if your opponent is in a hurry to give you $500 when he owes you only $50 . . . well, it's a lot to ask of some people, but being honest and returning the extra $450 pays off in good will and a reputation for honesty later on. Monopoly teaches us to accept favorable errors gracefully (like the Community Chest card which reads "Bank Error in Your Favor"), but never at the expense of another opponent.

One of the easiest money mistakes to commit is confusing $10 and $100 bills. Don't laugh, often a player will pay a $100 bill and two $1 bills for a $12 rent. There have been games where a player, knowing that one of his opponents constantly confused the two bills, made sure that opponent kept plenty of tens and hundreds on hand, and he asked for all his smaller rents in $10 bills. This is cutthroat to the point of poor sportsmanship. Win because of your own strength, not because of your opponent's petty visual weakness.

Do not forget to collect any money owed you, especially your Go salary. Many players are in such a hurry to move that they forget to ask for their money. Don't fall into the habit of asking for your Go money three turns after you pass. This will certainly win you no friends.

Make your opponents put their houses up neatly to avoid confusion as to which property has three houses and which has only two. When in doubt, demand that —since it is your opponent's fault that he didn't arrange his houses neatly—you should have to pay only the lower rent. He will straighten his houses up surprisingly quickly.

When you draw the Chance card which says "Make General Repairs on All Your Property. For Each House, Pay . . . ," be sure to count only your *own* houses and hotels. Don't hurt yourself any more than you have to. For that matter, read all Chance and Community Chest cards carefully. If it says "Advance Token to the Nearest Railroad," you can, and you *should*, buy that Railroad if it is unowned. In fact, whenever you draw a card which directs you to move your token to a property, you may buy that property if it is unowned, whether or not the card says you may.

Try to remember the general order of the Chance cards. These cards often send you places where you may not want to go, and are therefore a dangerous uncontrollable variable. However, after the original shuffle before the game, the cards always rotate *in the same order*. It's a good idea to make a mental note of which cards come before the "Advance Token to Boardwalk" and "Advance to Illinois Avenue" cards as the deck is run through for the first time. The knowledge that a crucial card is coming up next can be the clue that makes or breaks you.

Make sure that your doubles work for you. In many cases, especially early in the game, rolling doubles is a big advantage. Don't ever forget to roll again—you roll doubles only once out of every six turns! An easy way to remember to roll again is to announce aloud that doubles have been rolled whenever they appear. Calling your opponents' attention to the doubles ensures that someone will remind you to complete your turn and roll again.

Later in the game, it is an advantage to be in Jail, so most players will choose to wait until they roll doubles to get out. They can remain there for only two turns, however, and must move the number they roll on their third turn, whether or not it is doubles. Always keep a careful count of how many turns your opponents have spent in Jail. Every time they elect to stay, that is another turn that they could have been paying the rent at your hotels.

All of these things which may seem trivial when considered separately are important factors when taken together. It is true that there is not much skill involved in remembering to roll again whenever you throw doubles or in keeping your $10 and $100 bills separate, but your chances of winning are greatly improved if you pay attention to the game and follow these hints. Small precautions like these, when combined with powerful concepts, can add up to certain victory. However, a skillful player pays attention to all of the finer points as well as to the major strategies. Skillful wheeling and dealing are inadequate to make up for sloppiness and inattentiveness.

CHAPTER 3 SUMMARY

    I. The slightest edge.
   II. Pay attention to position.
   VI. Watch which properties are unowned.
  III. Watch your opponents' money and mortgaged properties.
  IV. Pay the right rents.
   V. Keep $10 and $100 bills separate.
 VII. Don't forget your Go money.
VIII. Keep the houses built neatly.
  IX. Make repairs on only your property.
   X. Know the general order of the Chance cards.
  XI. Roll again whenever you get doubles.
 XII. No life sentences.
XIII. The little things make a big difference.

CHAPTER 4

The Crucial Houses

How Mediterranean Avenue Can Be More Valuable Than Boardwalk

In a Monopoly game, just as in the real world, certain commodities react to the laws of *supply and demand.* For instance, if you wanted to sell a property in a private auction, the price which that property would command would depend on the demand for that property. In Monopoly, if it were a property which would complete a color group for another player, then that player would probably be willing to offer a high price for it. Since the supply of properties is limited (28), a property often has a "true value" which is well above its purchase price. The true value of any property changes from turn to turn, depending on what are commonly known as *market conditions.*

There are two conditions which determine the value of any commodity in a supply-and-demand situation:

1. Its usefulness to you. The fourth Railroad is most useful, and therefore most valuable, for a player with the other three Railroads.

2. The desire of another player to use that commodity against you. In a competitive game, a player will often buy what appears to be a worthless property, just to keep his opponent from getting it. The best defense is a good offense!

This chapter will consider how these principles of supply and demand apply to a crucial factor in every Monopoly game—*the houses.* The official rules restrict the supply of houses to 32. In addition, once color groups are completed, the demand for those houses is constantly high. Because of this restricted supply and high demand, the true value of a house is determined by the conditions described above.

But there are other factors in the official rules on housing which make this a very special type of supply-and-demand situation. Those factors are:

1. *The price of a house varies, depending on the color group for which it is bought.* A house on the Dark Blue group costs $200, whereas a house on the Purple group costs only $50.

2. *All houses, no matter what their purchase price, are taken from the* same *limited supply of 32 houses.*

3. *In case of a housing shortage, the available houses are auctioned off,* one by one, *and sold to the highest bidder.*

4. *A hotel is the equivalent of five houses, but ownership of a hotel does not* directly *change the supply of 32 houses.*

5. *When houses (or hotels) are sold back to the Bank, they must be sold in reverse of the order in which they were built.* This is the official Parker Brothers rule, and is often overlooked by many players. As you will see, it has many important implications.

6. *When houses (or hotels) are sold back to the Bank, they are sold for half their purchase price.*

With these factors in mind, we are ready to examine the strategies which can be applied to the housing market.

As any Monopoly player knows, the more houses that are built on a property, the higher the rent that can be collected from that property. Furthermore, a cheap color group with many houses collects more rent than an expensive color group with no houses. Finally, in every game of Monopoly, houses are built on color groups sooner or later (in skillful games, sooner!). These three points, taken together, lead logically to the first principle of housing manipulation:

IF THERE ARE NO HOUSES AVAILABLE FOR PURCHASE, ANY COLOR GROUP WHICH DOES

NOT ALREADY HAVE HOUSES IS TEMPORARI-
LY WORTHLESS. This principle is the basis for all
housing shortage strategies.

Chapter 1 introduced the concept of a "critical level"
of houses—the level of three houses on each property in
a color group. The addition of the third house causes the
rents to double, or even triple. Clearly, a color group
which is not at the critical level is no match for a color
group which is developed to that level, except in the
most extreme instances. For this reason, the second
principle of housing manipulation is necessary:

IF THERE ARE NOT ENOUGH HOUSES
AVAILABLE TO DEVELOP A COLOR GROUP TO
THE CRITICAL LEVEL, THEN THAT COLOR
GROUP IS WORTH VERY LITTLE AT THAT MO-
MENT. This principle can be used as an important
guide to your strategies of play. An expert has as his
goal to develop all his color groups, one at a time, to the
criticial level while doing all in his power to prevent his
opponents from developing their color groups to the
critical level. Housing shortage strategies are designed to
help him achieve that goal.

Because of the limited housing supply, it is obvious
that if a house is sitting on a property which you own, it
is "out of circulation" and is one less house which your
opponent can build on his own color group. If there are
plenty of houses available in the Bank, this fact is insignificant. But if you purchase the last two houses from
the Bank for $100 and put them on Mediterranean Ave-
nue and Baltic Avenue, you have stopped your opponents from doing any further building; perhaps you have
even kept them from reaching the critical level on their
color groups. The value of those houses is much greater
than the mere increase in rents on Mediterranean and
Baltic. The second condition of supply and demand
shows that the true value of those houses is determined
by how much damage they *could* have done if your opponents had had the opportunity to use them.

Here is a simple example (with rents given):

* * *

Mr. Expert	*Bob Boardwalker*
Mediterranean	Park Place
3 houses: $90	2 houses: $500
Baltic	Boardwalk
3 houses: $180	2 houses: $600

There are other color groups developed around the board, and the Bank has only two houses left for sale. Mr. Expert has several hundred dollars, but Bob Boardwalker has only $100. Mr. Expert buys the last two houses for $50 each (Bob doesn't have enough money to buy them at $200 each), and the situation looks like this:

Mr. Expert	*Bob Boardwalker*
Mediterranean	Park Place
4 houses: $160	2 houses: $500
Baltic	Boardwalk
4 houses: $320	2 houses: $600

By his $100 investment, Mr. Expert has done two things. He has increased the rent on his properties, and more importantly, he has made certain that unless someone sells houses back to the Bank, Bob will not be able to buy the additional house on each property which he needs to reach the critical level. To appreciate how important this second accomplishment is, look at what would have happened if Mr. Expert had let Bob accumulate some money and buy those two houses:

BEFORE

Mr. Expert	*Bob Boardwalker*
Mediterranean	Park Place
3 houses:$90	2 houses: $500
Baltic	Boardwalk
3 houses:$180	2 houses: $600

AFTER

Mr. Expert	*Bob Boardwalker*
Mediterranean	Park Place
3 houses: $90	3 houses: $1100
Baltic	Boardwalk
3 houses: $180	3 houses: $1400

Before, Mr. Expert might have been able to afford a land on Boardwalk or Park Place. Now, by refusing to invest the $100 to "soak up" the last two houses, he has allowed the rents on the Dark Blue group to more than double! He has, by his inaction, *permitted* Bob to reach the critical level. A land on Park Place or Boardwalk now would be fatal. The process of soaking up houses would have saved his life. The true value of those last two houses was not the $100 which he could have paid for them, but closer to five or six times that amount.

More than the importance of soaking up can be learned from this example. The element of timing is also a vital housing principle. Suppose that Mr. Expert had decided to soak up the houses, but to wait several truns to do so. Assume further that during that waiting period Bob Boardwalker passes Go and collects some other rents, giving him the $400 which he needs to buy those houses. Now it is not so easy for Mr. Expert to soak up houses. Since Bob wants the houses too, the players want more than the Bank has available to sell, and the Bank must hold an auction for the two available houses. Bob must legally start the bidding at $200 for each house, since that is the minimum amount he is permitted to pay. This means that if Mr. Expert wants to soak up those houses, he must bid more than Bob, or over $200 for each house! Even if he has the money, Mr. Expert must ask himself how valuable that house-soaking power is, since he will be putting those houses on Mediterranean and Baltic, places from which it will take a long time to recover his investment. His delay has cost him dearly!

It is not unusual in this sort of situation for the owner of a cheaper color group to find himself forced to sit by helplessly, unable to try to outbid the owners of higher-priced color groups in a housing shortage. In general:

OWNERS OF EXPENSIVE COLOR GROUPS OFTEN HAVE AN ADVANTAGE IN HOUSING AUCTIONS, AS THEIR HIGHER MINIMUM PRICE FOR HOUSES CAN TAKE THE AUCTION FAR OUT OF THE RANGE OF PRICES WHICH THE OWNERS OF CHEAPER COLOR GROUPS COULD PROFITABLY AFFORD.

The rule for the timing of house-soaking is:

Don't be a mouse. Soak up the house.

After understanding the importance of the housing market, it is time to explore the way in which this market relates to the role of hotels in a Monopoly game and the way the rules concerning hotels can affect your housing strategies.

According to the official rules, a player may build a hotel only after he has four houses on each property of a complete color group. In fact, he must actually erect those houses first, and then return them to the Bank to receive the hotel. This procedural technicality has far-reaching consequences for the player who understands how to exploit it.

The direct implication of this requirement is:

NO PLAYER MAY BUILD HOTELS UNLESS THERE ARE ENOUGH HOUSES AVAILABLE TO FIRST PUT FOUR ON EACH PROPERTY IN THE COLOR GROUP. A PLAYER MAY NOT "BYPASS" A HOUSING SHORTAGE BY BUILDING HOTELS. For example, if you own the Orange group and already have two houses on each property, the correct procedure for building hotels would be:

1. Compute how many houses are necessary for you to reach the level of four houses on each property $(2 + 2 + 2 = 6)$.

2. Buy those houses and erect them on your properties (houses are $100 each, and $6 \times \$100 = \$600$).

3. Return to the Bank four houses and $100 for *each*

hotel you wish to buy. In this case, that would cost an additional $300.

4. Place the hotels on your properties.

Why take the trouble to erect four houses on each property if you're only going to return them to the Bank two seconds later? If the Bank has plenty of houses, it's really not necessary to go through the motions of buying the houses and returning them. But if there are not enough houses to complete Step 2, then a player may not go on to Step 3, and he cannot build hotels.

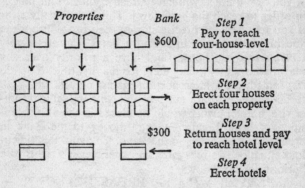

HOTEL BUILDING

The correct four-step procedure for building from the two-house level to the hotel level on the Orange group.

Furthermore, the technical procedure for building will be very important later when we discuss the correct procedure for *selling* hotels back to the Bank.

The limit of 32 houses, when considered together with the "reverse-order" rule mentioned in the list of six factors given earlier in this chapter, has important strategic implications regarding hotels. The reverse-order rule states that a player may sell his hotels either *all at once* or *one house at a time* (one hotel equals five houses), *in reverse of the manner in which they were erected*. If he sells *only one house from each property*, he can absorb four houses on each property—his hotels turn into four houses each. By doing this, he can put a tremendous drain on the housing supply and prevent other players from developing to the critical level. By breaking down his hotels, a player can often dry up the housing market at any time he wishes!

Furthermore, a player can break his hotels down in this manner, even if other players want to buy those houses. The housing shortage rule says that a housing shortage exists if two or more players wish to *buy* more houses than are available. The key word here is "buy." If you own a hotel, you have already bought four houses in order to reach the hotel level. This is especially clear if you followed the precise step-by-step procedure when you built the hotels. In selling a hotel, you are clearly *reclaiming* those houses and have a priority over any player who wants to buy them for the first time. You are not forced to bid in an auction against players who wish to buy, since you are not buying—you are selling! Otherwise, a hotel owner would be placed in the absurb position of being required to *pay* money to the Bank in order to *sell* his hotels to the Bank. To avoid this ridiculous situation, we recognize the hotel owner's rights to a "priority of breakdown":

A PLAYER WHO IS "BREAKING DOWN" A HOTEL TO FOUR HOUSES HAS PRIORITY OVER ANY PLAYERS WHO WISHES TO BUY THOSE HOUSES. Mr. Expert will immediately perceive the power of the priority of breakdown. A player could build hotels on a cheap color group and wait patiently until his opponents were ready to build to the critical level on their own color group. Then, BOOM! He could break his hotels down to four houses on each property, collect half the purchase price of the "fifth houses" from the Bank, and deprive his opponents of those desperately needed houses. If they then attempted to build straight to hotels, he could cite the appropriate rules which demonstrate that this sort of "bypassing" is illegal. You can be sure that there will be a lot of screaming and yelling when players realize that Mr. Expert has beaten them through his superior knowledge of the intricacies of the rules, but rules are rules.

One final word on priority of breakdown. The question sometimes arises of what would happen if two players, each with hotels, wanted to soak up the last four houses in the Bank. In this case, standard procedure is to have an auction for each block of four houses. The player who bids the most money for the right of first breakdown may then break down one hotel. The auction continues until all of the Bank's lots of four houses have been sold.

The reverse-order rule has still another implication, one which can be even more devastating than the first. This delicate loophole actually makes it a risk to buy hotels at all!

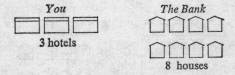

The reverse-order rule states that you must sell your hotels in reverse of the manner in which you put them up. In this chapter, the exact manner in which hotels were erected was discussed. Let's try to reverse that order in this position. In Step 3, it was required that to buy a hotel you return four houses to the Bank with enough money to pay for a "fifth house." To reverse this, you must return your hotels to the Bank one at a time and receive four houses for each one. This works fine for the first two hotels. But then you reach this position:

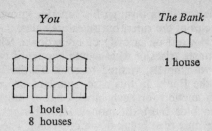

The Bank can't return four houses to you for your last hotel, so you can't break it down any further. You're stuck! If you wanted to sell the hotels, you would have to sell them *in their entirety.*

Let's examine the same position, only this time, let's give the Bank 12 houses, as follows:

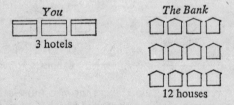

Now, you can complete the reversal of Step 3 and return all your hotels to the Bank, receiving $150 ($50 for each returned hotel), and reaching the following position:

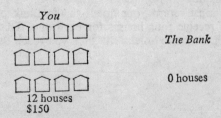

Since you have successfully completed the reversal of Step 3 in the building process, you may now continue to sell houses one by one, in reverse of the manner in which you built them. By selling three more houses (one from each property), you will receive an additional $150 and achieve your desired final position:

You			The Bank
⌂	⌂	⌂	⌂
⌂	⌂	⌂	⌂
⌂	⌂	⌂	⌂
9 houses			3 houses
$300			

The only difference between the two positions is the number of houses in the Bank. In the first example, all three hotels would have to be sold for half price; in the second example, you could sell exactly as many houses as you need to. Being forced to sell three hotels for half price involves a tremendous financial loss.

This is called the "hotel trap." The reason for the name is clear. If a player has hotels on his properties during a housing shortage, he is trapped into keeping his hotels if he wants to avoid major financial loss. While the housing shortage remains in effect (or as long as fewer than 12 houses are in the Bank), he may not raise cash by selling his buildings unless he wishes to sell all of his hotels, in their entirety.

Although hotels provide higher rents than do four houses, hotel owners run the risk of being trapped. It's an all-or-nothing situation, and when you're forced to sell for half price, it's a situation which is financially unacceptable to the experienced player. The difference in rent between four houses and a hotel is in many cases insufficient to compensate for the added risk.

If a player always stops at four houses and never succumbs to the temptation to build hotels, he will never be caught in the hotel trap and will always be able to raise money gradually by selling one house at a time. He has no worries about turning hotels into four houses, since he always has those four houses to begin with. In addition, a player who never builds hotels will never have to go through the problems of logically explaining the reasons for the doctrine of priority of breakdown to his opponents. Finally, he can always flood the housing market with houses whenever he finds it necessary, by building as many hotels as he sees fit. (Of course, he will do this only when he needs to put the houses on his other color groups and is sure that he has enough money to control most of the houses which he releases.)

So the general rule for hotels is:

DO NOT BUILD HOTELS ON A COLOR GROUP UNLESS YOU ARE SURE THAT YOU WILL BE ABLE TO BREAK THOSE HOTELS DOWN TO FOUR HOUSES EACH WHENEVER THE NEED MIGHT ARISE.

What are the tactical implications of the housing rules which you can use to your advantage in the very next game you play?

1. Build to the critical level and keep your opponents from doing so.

2. Make sure that you reach the critical level on one color group before you start to develop the next one.

3. Tie up as many houses as possible, even if only to keep your opponents from getting them.

4. If you build hotels, keep a close eye on the housing market, and if there is *any* danger of the development of a housing shortage, *break down to four houses immediately.* (If there is a fight over the houses which you are soaking up, explain the doctrine of priority of breakdown.)

5. If your opponents have built hotels and they are low on cash, it is a good idea to buy enough houses to make it impossible for them to gradually sell their hotels. In effect, you are setting the hotel trap for your opponents. This can turn a lost game into a winning one.

6. Never let your opponents bypass a housing shortage by building illegally to hotels.

7. If you need to make houses available for use on another color group, do so by building *up* to hotels. This will release houses from those properties. Also be sure that you have enough money to control the houses which you release. Your opponents may want those houses too, and force an auction.

By use of the fine points in the housing rules and a knowledge of the factors which influence the behavior of the housing market, an informed player obtains a powerful edge over his less knowledgeable opponents. No amount of luck can change what the rules say, and you've got the rules in the palm of your hand.

CHAPTER 4 SUMMARY

I. True value determined by:
    A. Usefulness to you.
    B. Usefulness to other players.
II. Six special features of the housing situation.
III. Color groups are worthless without houses.
IV. Soaking up.
V. Timing.
VI. Advantages of expensive color groups in auctions.
VII. You can't bypass a housing shortage.
VIII. Priority of breakdown.
IX. The hotel trap.
X. Tactical tips.

Investment Analysis for Funds and Profits

Many people ask, "What is the best color group to own?" You would be amazed at how difficult it sometimes is to convince people of the fact that *no single color group can be called better than any other if the position in the game is unknown.* Pulling two color groups out of the context of a game and calling one better than the other is as meaningless and foolish as quoting a few words out of the context of an entire speech. Mr. Expert knows how the general circumstances of a game determine the changing values of color groups. Market conditions can make something valuable today and worthless tomorrow.

It is essential that a player understand the basic principles of investment analysis if he hopes to become a winning player. Without a basic knowledge of what makes a color group valuable at a given time in a given situation, he will be fooled time and again by players who offer deals which look good on the surface, but are rotten inside. This chapter analyzes the basic principles of investment analysis. By applying these principles, a player can accurately gauge the immediate and potential values of color groups. Trades are a combination of dollars and sense.

This chapter introduces the "changing value" theory of color groups. It also details the five vital questions which Mr. Expert asks about every position, how the answers to those questions can make *any* color group into a lethal weapon, and the ways in which Mr. Expert compares color groups in light of their possibilities for exploitation.

The first principle of investment analysis is a simple one:

ANY COLOR GROUP IS BETTER THAN NO COLOR GROUP. The utilities and Railroads bring you nice Christmas bonuses, and ownership of four Railroads is nothing to sneeze at, but these properties simply do not have the power of color groups (if you are unfamiliar with the board, the Railroads and utilities are not color properties). Use this principle to your advantage in proposing trades. You will find that many players have a warped fascination for utilities or Railroads and might be willing to give up a color group or some key trading properties to get them. Just be careful that *you* don't flush your money down the Water Works.

The second principle of investment analysis is the "changing value" theory itself. Its underlying precept is that:

ALL COLOR GROUPS *CHANGE* IN VALUE OVER THE COURSE OF A GAME, DEPENDING ON THE FINANCIAL AND STRATEGIC POSITIONS OF THE OWNER AND THE OTHER PLAYERS, AND ON THE AVAILABLE HOUSING SUPPLY.

Why do you need a changing value theory? To show how questions like the following two have very different answers in different situations:

1. Which are more valuable, the Light Blues or the Yellows?

Situation A: If you have $2500, the Yellows are better—you can develop them fully and they pack a more potent punch.

Situation B: If you have only $600, and the Bank has only 12 houses left, the Light Blues are better. You can tie up all 12 houses on the Light Blues, a much more helpful tactic than spreading only four houses over the Yellows (houses cost $150 on the Yellows, $50 on the Light Blues).

2. Which are more valuable, the Oranges or the Dark Blues?

Situation A: If you have $1200 and the Bank has only six houses, the Dark Blues are better—they can be built to their devastating critical level, whereas the Oranges (a three-property color group) cannot.

Situation B: If you have $1200 and the Bank has 12 houses, most experts would take the Oranges because of the fairly equal *total* rent ($750/750/800 and $1100/1400) and the opportunity to absorb twice as many houses.

As you can see, a color group's value is subject to a wide variety of conditions. But given a specific set of conditions, how does Mr. Expert estimate the relative value of two different color groups?

To compare a series of advantages, it is first necessary to decide very clearly in your own mind what it is that you are comparing. This is the reason for the third principle of investment analysis:

UNDERSTAND THE DIFFERENT ADVANTAGES TO BE DERIVED FROM OWNING ANY COLOR GROUP:
1. BANKRUPTING POWER.
2. HOUSE-SOAKING POWER.
3. PROFIT-EARNING POWER.
4. GLAMOUR POWER.

We will explore each of these advantages in detail and show which color groups have more of these advantages in which situations.

The first advantage is BANKRUPTING POWER. Because bankruptcy is the key to victory, bankrupting power is essential to the assessment of the value of any given color group in a given situation. This power is a measure of how deadly it is for a player to land on the color group when it is fully developed. Since the highest possible rent on a property is the rent with a hotel, bankrupting power of any color group is computed by examining the rent with a hotel on the most expensive property in the color group. The Dark Blue group has the most bankrupting power; the Purple group has the least.

Since the only way to win the game is by bankrupting the other players, bankruptcy underlies almost any strategy, either directly or indirectly. Therefore, it is according to bankrupting power that the novice player mistakenly values his color groups at all times. But this is a horrendous error! Bankrupting power is not the only advantage which a color group offers. It is only a single standard by which to measure a color group's value. It does not take into account such critical aspects of the game as house-building costs and the frequency with which people land on the color group. Mr. Expert uses bankrupting power as a tool for measurement, not as the sole measure of a color group.

The second advantage is HOUSE-SOAKING POWER. This is the ability of a color group to absorb houses and to control the housing market, as described in Chapter 4. A color group's house-soaking power is determined by two factors:

1. The price of houses. Color groups with low building costs are ideal for soaking up houses. At only $50 or $100 for each house, the first four color groups after Go have strong house-soaking power.

2. The maximum number of houses that can be built on the color group. Since color groups consist of either two or three properties, this affects how well you will be able to control the housing market. Thus, the Light Blues have more house-soaking power than do the Purples, as they can soak up four more houses for only $50 apiece. It is important to note that with any two color groups in his possession, a player could monopolize 50–67% of the total available houses. And after all, the game is Monopoly!

* * *

The third advantage is PROFIT-EARNING POWER. This is the power of a color group to bring you more money for each dollar you invest in improving it. This advantage is related to the amount of money you have available to invest, since a cheap color group at the critical level will bring you more money than an expensive color group with two houses on each property. In general, the more money you put in, the more you get out.

The profit-earning power of a color group is a measure of the speed with which a player recovers the money he invests in developing the properties. The faster the color group returns your investment, the sooner you can look forward to earning profits. Obviously, your opponents will have to land on your color group if you plan to make any money from it. For this reason, profit-earning power is related to the probability that an opponent will land on any property in your color group on any turn.

The mathematical details are unimportant, but a general knowledge of the odds of landing on a color group can be important. The following is a list of all the color groups in the order of the probability of landing on each one:

> *Most Probable:* Oranges
> Reds
> Yellows
> Greens
> Maroons
> Light Blues
> Dark Blues
> *Least Probable:* Purples

According to this list, the Light Blues are landed on more often than are the Dark Blues. Does this mean that the Light Blues have a higher profit-earning power? Definitely not!! To determine profit-earning power, you must also consider the amount of rent collected whenever a player lands on the color group. A player may not land on Boardwalk very often, but when he does, it's expensive!

Therefore, we have used a computer to simulate tens of thousands of rolls of the dice in a Monopoly game, and we have computed the order of the color groups' profit-earning powers at different levels of investment. Keeping in mind that profit-earning power is only one aspect of the value of a color group, here is a list of color groups in order of profit-earning power:

NUMBER OF DOLLARS INVESTED IN HOUSES

Profit-Earning Power	*$500*	*$1000*	*$1500*	*$2000*	*$2500+*
MOST	Light Blues	Oranges	Oranges	Dark Blues	Greens
	Purples	Dark Blues	Yellows	Oranges	Yellows
	Oranges	Maroons	Dark Blues	Yellows	Reds
	Maroons	Light Blues	Reds	Reds	Dark Blues
	Dark Blues	Yellows	Maroons	Greens	Oranges
	Yellows	Greens	Greens	Maroons	Maroons
	Greens	Reds	Light Blues	Light Blues	Light Blues
LEAST	Reds	Purples	Purples	Purples	Purples

As you can see, the profit-earning power of any color group changes, depending on how much money you have available to invest. This is precisely as the changing value theory would predict. In general, the most valuable color group in terms of profit-earning power is that group on which you can afford to build straight to the critical level.

While we're inspecting this chart, we should dispel some old wives' tales about the profitability of some color groups:

a. If you have a lot of money to invest ($2500+), there are three better color groups in which to put your money than those Dark Blues with the infamous Board-walk.

b. At times, those two cheap Purple properties are actually the second most profitable color group on the board.

c. The Yellow group is always more profitable than the Red group, even though the Reds are landed on more often than the Yellows.

d. If you don't have too much cash, the Oranges are the most profitable place to put your money.

Profit-earning power is a very important measure in the estimation of the value of a color group.

The fourth and final advantage of a color group is GLAMOUR POWER. Why will a lot of people pay a lot of money to see a movie with Robert Redford or Cybill Shepherd, even if the movie doesn't get excellent reviews? The glamour of these movie stars is enough to make people want to see the movies, no matter how good those movies really are. Monopoly has its movie stars too! Many players find certain color groups more glamorous than others. They are willing to give up a lot for these color groups, whether or not they are really valuable in the situation in question.

Glamour power is a highly subjective value which you can alter by the way you speak of the different color groups in any given game. It can be determined only by psyching out your opponents to discover if they have any hidden preferences or prejudices about color groups. In most novice games, the Greens and Dark Blues have very high glamour power (as do the Railroads). Some players would trade their families' jewels for Boardwalk; other players really love to play engineer on the Railroads. But after all, most players do not have the benefit of the profit-earning power table which you just saw, and do not understand how the value of a color group changes as the game progresses.

It is up to you to use your powers of observation to discover just how much glamour power a color group has in any given game. Once you discover what your opponents prefer, you can offer them what they want, but on your own terms. Most opponents do not have the will power to resist their favorite properties.

Knowing the four advantages which a color group can provide, how do you pick the best color group for your specific needs? This is a very difficult question to answer in detail. There are no hard-and-fast rules which can tell a player that he should *definitely* take the Orange group instead of the Yellow group. After all, the Oranges are better for house-soaking, while the Yellows are better for bankrupting, but the Oranges return your investment faster for smaller investments, and on and on. Even experts will disagree on which property groups are better in the same set of circumstances. The only thing that is certain when making a judgment about a color group is that there is always room for intelligent disagreement.

Yet, even with many possible "correct" opinions, there *are* some objective measures that all players can use to make comparisons. There are definite reasons why we can confidently state that, except in the most severe economic depressions, Boardwalk and Park Place are definitely better than Mediterranean and Baltic if you are looking for a color group which will give you a balanced attack early in the game. The Dark Blues are clearly superior in three of the four power categories. Their only major weakness is their inability to be used for rapid house-soaking. Unless we were interested only in soaking up houses, the Dark Blues would clearly be more advantageous than the Purples.

But once we compare color groups that are not total opposites, all-encompassing generalizations are no longer possible. The specific circumstances must be taken into account, and the weight assigned to each advantage or disadvantage of a color group varies with those circumstances. The manner in which the situation shapes a color group's value is summarized in the fourth principle of investment analysis:

* * *

A COLOR GROUP'S VALUE TO YOU IS DE-
TERMINED AT ANY MOMENT BY YOUR ABILI-
TY TO EXPLOIT ITS PARTICULAR ADVAN-
TAGES.

Since there are four basic advantages to owning a col-
or group, a player must judge whether the color group
he is considering will provide him with the advantages
he needs. Then, he must decide whether he can make
full use of those advantages if he has them at his disposal. For example, if you wanted to soak up the last 10
houses because your opponent was about to build on the
Greens, you would look for a color group such as the
Light Blues. If you had enough cash on hand and you
owned the Light Blues, you could meet your objectives.
In this case, you would be able to exploit the advantages
of the Light Blues—advantages which would help your
position—so they would be very valuable to you.

Similarly, if you had lots of cash, but there were no
houses left in the Bank, you would not be able to exploit
the high profit-earning power of the Yellow group.
Thus, in a housing shortage situation, the Yellows
should be regarded as being worth very little at the moment. If you don't have the ability to end the housing
shortage, you can be sure that your opponents are not
going to cooperate and release houses for you to build.
The Yellows would be strictly a speculative long-term
investment.

Unfortunately, there is no easy way to instantly evaluate how well you can exploit the advantages of a color
group at a given moment, taking into account all of the
necessary psychological factors (this is why computers
cannot play the game as well as people, yet). There are,
however, several basic positional questions which you
should *always* ask yourself whenever you estimate your
power to exploit a color group. Any time you rate your
position (which should be often), ask yourself:

*1. How many other color groups have been built to
the critical level? How many could be built to that level
on this turn?*

2. Is there a housing shortage?

3. How much money do I have?

4. How much money do my opponents have?

5. In what ways could the game drastically change its character as a result of one roll of the dice (for example, a key unbought property, a jackpot square, an expensive rent?)

It is obviously impossible to show precisely how the answer to each question will tell you how well you can exploit a specific advantage of a specific color group. That is not the purpose of these questions. Rather, the answers to these questions, when taken together, will give you a general knowledge of what are the most important variables in the game at that moment.

Each question by itself can, however, serve as a general barometer of certain trends in the game. For instance, if your answer to the first question is that very few color groups are well developed, then you are probably in a fairly "young" game. It would take several setbacks to seriously hurt any player's position in the game. For this reason, you can afford to acquire a slightly more expensive color group, one whose profit-earning power is not the best for you yet. You know that you will have time to accumulate more money over the next few turns without being forced to pay any large rents. This extra cash would give you enough money to build to the critical level on your more expensive color group and allow you to best exploit the profit-earning power and bankrupting power of your position.

Your answer to the second question is also an important indicator. If there is a housing shortage, then the value of any new color group (or any undeveloped color group) is in immediate jeopardy. If you have any immediate hopes of exploiting the profit-earning power of that color group, you will need another source of houses that you can make available for your new color group. Don't forget, your opponents' hotels can be broken down to grab what appear to be available houses. Do you have enough cash to withstand a bidding war if an auction is necessary? If you aren't sure that you have a means of getting houses, a new color group's profit-earning power is unexploitable, and so is its bankrupting power. Don't trade all of your property away for a Marvin Gardens which can never bloom.

The answer to how much cash you have available to invest is the most obvious general indicator of how well you can exploit the advantages of any color group. The earlier table clearly demonstrated that the amount of cash available for investment directly affects the profit-earning power of any color group. This is only a general indicator, however, because your cash can be increased in an emergency by the methods which will be explained in Chapter 14, or just as easily wiped out by bad luck. For now, realize that in a game with a lot of developed color groups, you will need a $300–500 *cushion* to survive minor difficulties. If you are forced to destroy all of your margin of safety to properly develop a color group, you are probably taking on more than you can handle. Even a small rent could make your houses come tumbling down even faster than they went up, and you'll be much the poorer for it. Therefore, the amount of cash on hand is an important indicator of how well you will be able to exploit the advantages of a color group.

The amount of cash available to your opponents will also help to guide your attitude toward which color groups would be most helpful to your position. If your opponents are poor and have traded to gain complete color groups, the middle-priced color groups are attractive to you for their easily exploited profit-earning power. Assuming you have a moderate amount of cash, you should be able to beat your opponents before they are able to develop to the critical level. A color group with moderate rents, when properly developed, could keep them from ever getting off the ground. On the other hand, if your opponents are powerful, you will need a more expensive color group with a high profit-earning power for larger investments, in order to fight back. The power of your opponents should play a major role in your decisions.

The final question is a measure of the explosiveness of the game. How has the game been so far? Are the houses constantly being built and torn down again? Has there been a lot of trading and screaming? Have large sums of money changed hands fairly regularly? If so, then your game is relatively unstable. If things have been relatively calm, then you can afford to relax—you're in a fairly stable game. A good test of the game's stability for you is to ask yourself, "How many bad rolls can I afford before things begin to get tough?" If your answer is one or two, the game is unstable. Any more and the game is peaceful.

Why know the game's stability? You guessed it! Because changes in stability, like most other things, affect the values of the various color groups. In a highly stable game, profit-earning power and house-soaking power are at a premium, and your ability to exploit the advantages of any color group can be measured fairly reliably from your cash on hand. In a game subject to wild swings in several directions, bankrupting power is at a premium, and everything should be geared toward exploiting that advantage to the utmost. If someone's about to go broke, make sure it's to you!

That's investment analysis in a nutshell. You are now able to tell, to some degree, how much a color group can help you in a situation. The next chapter deals with strategy—how to merge your helpful color groups into a coordinated attack.

CHAPTER 5 SUMMARY

   I. The "best" color group.
  II. The "changing value" theory.
 III. Color group advantages:
      A. Bankrupting power.
      B. House-soaking power.

    C. Profit-earning power.
    D. Glamour power.
IV. Value is limited by your ability to exploit advantages.
 V. Position evaluation questions.

Strategy Selection, or Planning Your Plunder

The preceding chapter should have put to rest any question as to a "best" color group. The best color group at any time is dependent on the situation. The game is constantly changing, especially when properties are still unowned. It is this same constant change of conditions which makes selecting a strategy during the game a difficult and often unreliable procedure. Surely there is no strategy which will be better than all others at all times.

Using a strategy can help us keep our goals and objectives clearly in mind. Since our strategy is always subject to immediate revision, it does not constitute a rigid plan of play. Rather, its purpose is to force us to plan ahead, anticipate likely situations, and prepare our reactions to those situations. Strategies are kept in mind and used as general guidelines for trading and developing. For that reason, a player who knows fairly well what he wants to do will have an edge over his opponents who do not. It is important to remain constantly alert while playing, and any plan, no matter how temporary, helps us to stay sharp.

There are several fundamental principles that are involved in selecting a strategy. All good players begin each game with essentially the same plan of attack: to buy all of the properties they can and to get a complete color group as quickly as possible, in order to knock out their opponents. However, players rapidly diverge from this strategy after the first few trips around the board. Trading soon becomes the only alternative for the player who wants to get a color group by means other than luck. This is the point where strategy considerations become very important. Here are the five fundamental principles that must be understood and adhered to throughout the game.

ANY GOOD STRATEGY IS GOOD ONLY AS LONG AS THE CONDITIONS ON WHICH THE STRATEGY IS BASED REMAIN CONSTANT.

For example, suppose your strategy is to lure your opponent into giving up several cheap color groups for one powerful, but hard-to-develop color group. You plan to be able to tie up enough houses and charge enough medium-size rents to prevent him from ever building up that powerful group against you. This strategy is good as long as your opponent cannot afford to build quickly to the critical level. If he somehow manages to obtain a large amount of money, you must shift your plan of attack, and fast! Why? Because one of the basic conditions on which your strategy is based is your opponent's lack of money, and that no longer exists. In this case, it may be too late to do anything. This leads to an important corollary to the first principle:

Try to select strategies which depend on the fewest varying conditions. The more variables there are, the greater the likelihood that something will go wrong.

ALL STRATEGIES REVOLVE AROUND PROPERTY ACQUISITION—EITHER THROUGH BANKRUPTCY OR THROUGH ACCEPTANCE OF PROPERTY IN LIEU OF RENT.

Since you hope to be the first to bankrupt other players, the immediate aims of all your strategies fall into one of two categories:

a. To stop other players from building while you develop and improve your own position (a "holding strategy").

b. To outbuild and overpower your opponent by sheer force (an "aggressive strategy").

Obviously, the importance of timing should not be underestimated when selecting your plan for snatching your opponents' properties. Keep in mind too that all strategies rely on property *development* to be successful. Having color groups without a sufficient flow of cash to build correctly is a disastrous error. It is rather difficult to convince another player to give you a property when you owe *him* rent. Developing property is the only way to acquire more property. Remember, a player with $10,000 cash and no color groups on which to build will lose very quickly if he doesn't buy some property. The biggest lakes run dry without rain.

STRATEGIES ARE A COMPROMISE BETWEEN WHAT YOU WANT AND WHAT YOU CAN GET.

By using a strategy and understanding what makes that strategy work, you stand a much better chance of getting exactly what you want. But as you have seen, strategy selection must be based on the conditions at the moment. If, for some reason, you want to own the Dark Blue group, but Boardwalk and Park Place are owned by two other players, your chances of acquiring that color group are slim. Undoubtedly, you could form a strategy to trade with each player in order to acquire the necessary property, but such a strategy would be very risky. You might get Park Place and then discover that the player who owns Boardwalk doesn't want to trade. Then you'd be stuck holding the place (Park Place, that is). It would be much smarter to use properties which you already own and to attempt to improve your position from that base. This leads to the next principle:

AIM YOUR STRATEGY AT SOMETHING THAT WILL PROVIDE IMMEDIATE ASSIST-ANCE IF YOU CAN GET IT.

Remember that your first and foremost concern is to stay alive in the game (dead men reap no rents). If you are trying to bankrupt somebody by making trades against him, he had better have some properties that will help your position immediately. Long-range plans are a luxury in a Monopoly game. If your opponent has the third Yellow property and he won't sell it or trade it, then you must force him to give it to you. If you are successful, then the immediate benefit will be the completion of the Yellow group for you. You are pursuing a property which will provide immediate improvement of your position—a wise objective. Although it is sometimes necessary to trade for a property, just so that you can turn around and trade it away, it is much safer to try to obtain something which has direct and immediate value to you. The laws of supply and demand are sometimes very fickle, and properties are often valuable only because they are valuable to an opponent. In such cases, you may be forced to rely heavily on the assumption that your opponent will trade. In general, however, when forming a strategy it is *preferable* to aim for things which can help directly to improve your position, independent of the activities of the other players.

KNOW WHAT SPECIFIC OCCURRENCES WILL FORCE YOU TO ABANDON YOUR STRATEGY.

A captain always knows when to abandon ship. A strategy is a very touchy thing. You may be counting on a player not to build houses on his properties, or you may be relying on a certain property to remain unowned for a little while longer. Whatever the situation, it is important to be aware of the potential problems which might arise as a result of a single action. In these cases, unlike the uncontrollable conditions described in the first principle, it is possible to bring psychological weapons into play to prevent such occurrences. If a player is about to spend money to build houses that would upset your plans, discourage him! Keep in mind at all times that you have the power to influence the game through your conversation. Always seek to minimize the possibilities of something upsetting your strategy. The numerous psychological weapons at your disposal will be explained in later chapters. For now, be aware that some smooth talking at the right moment can save an entire strategy.

* * *

How can these fundamental principles be applied? Just as in investment analysis, there are many different factors which Mr. Expert weighs when selecting a temporary strategy. He asks himself such questions as: "What is the financial position of the other players?" "Can I afford to build to the critical level on the color groups I am interested in?" "Who owns the key properties in my strategy?" "Are there any immediate threats on the board right now?" "If my opponents have a big advantage in cash, will stalling help me catch up?" "Is it possible for me to stall trading?" "Is there a housing shortage?" "If not, can I create a housing shortage?" The answers to these questions shape the expert's decision as to which direction his strategy should take.

When are most strategy decisions made?

a. When a color group is completed ("Should I wait, trade, or build?").

b. When a trade is offered.

c. When your opponents prepare to trade in a way which can harm your position (most trades between opponents are harmful).

Such times of decision do not come too often, and mistakes at these critical moments are often irreparable. Games among experts are won or lost because of a player's ability or inability to make the correct strategy decision about a once-in-a-game chance ("Should I accept that trade?"). When making a decision, a player must take all of the factors detailed earlier in this chapter into consideration. Then he must evaluate what appears to be the best course of action.

There are four general types of strategies. Although most strategies in individual games are combinations of these strategies, these are a close approximation to an accurate classification of the thousands of possible plans of attack which can be successfully employed to make the most of a situation. They are intended to be a general outline of what a player can be seeking during a Monopoly game.

* * *

THE QUICK KAYO (the Atomic Bomb Strategy). This strategy is very risky, especially if other color groups are developed by your opponents. It is usually used only if:

a. you are *desperate* to bankrupt another player or to force him to tear down his deadly hotels, or

b. you have only one color group and have no choice but to develop quickly to prevent your opponents from acquiring enough money to develop their color groups.

This strategy is usually implemented by mortgaging all unnecessary properties and using *all* your cash to leap to the four-house or hotel level. The element of timing in this strategy is vital. You must take your opponents by surprise, and it is usually most effective if one (or more) of your opponents is six, seven, or eight squares before your color group. Just before he rolls, ask that the dice be held and announce, "Wait a minute! I want to build."

Then, pump *everything you have* into building as high as possible. Don't worry about your cash cushion—if this fails, you haven't any hope anyway. Obviously, the greater the bankrupting power of your color group, the more likely you will be to succeed. This strategy is also most effective if your opponents have relatively little cash on hand.

If there are no other developed color groups on the board, then the Quick Kayo is obviously quite safe. This is rarely the time such a strategy is employed, however. Usually, it is used when the situation has forced you to trade away your chance at a color group with high profit-earning power because your opponents have been maneuvering to keep you from getting any color group at all. Your objective in this strategy is to gain the necessary properties to switch your attack to a more stable, long-term strategy. If you are successful, you have salvaged a poor position and given yourself excellent winning chances. The risk is high, however, and the more your opponents have developed their color groups, the riskier this strategy is, because *you have no cash cushion.*

The Quick Kayo is really no more than an accelerated version of the general principle of building as fast as possible. The major difference is that the Quick Kayo is a no-holds-barred, caution-to-the-winds strategy. The principle of building early is not nearly so risky, since you keep a cash cushion, and is always correct procedure.

THE HOUSING HOARD (the Ho-Ho Strategy). Several earlier examples have demonstrated the power of this strategy. It is most effective when you own two or more cheap color groups and your strongest opponent does not have the money to develop his more expensive color group right away. It will take him some time to build to the critical level (assuming he knows to build to that point), and during that time you can move to soak up as many houses as you possibly can to create a housing shortage. This strategy, like the Quick Kayo, is a race against time. The object is to be the first to buy as many of the available houses as possible, even if it requires mortgaging and depleting your cash reserves.

Your chances of success are greatest when one of your other opponents also has a relatively cheap color group, on which he has built moderately, but not quite to the critical level. Between the two of you, your goal is to tie up at least 26 houses, leaving only six for your dangerous opponent with the expensive color group. It is usually easiest to tie up so many houses if your opponent is unaware of the rules concerning housing shortages. Many players have no idea that a housing shortage will prevent them from building, so don't be surprised if your opponent sits back complacently while you buy all of the houses!

Once you have absorbed as many houses as possible, it is no longer important that your opponent owns a color group with more profit-earning power. He will not be able to exploit it. As long as you control the housing market, your medium-sized rents will effectively drain your opponents' money. Without houses, they will be unable to replenish the cash being drained from their

positions. You bankrupt your most powerful opponent
first, and use the properties you acquire from him against
your other opponents. Patience, and victory is yours.

THE BRUTE FORCE BATTLE (the Muhammad
Ali Strategy). This is the simplest and most common of
all the strategies. Your plan is to develop color groups
with higher profit-earning power than your opponents',
and then to outslug them with your more intelligent investments and higher rents. What could be easier? This
strategy is most effective if you have two color groups
built to the critical level. Many deadly winning combinations include one expensive color group and one
cheaper color group. The strategy is to use the revenues
from the less expensive color group (which has high
profit-earning power for small investments) in order to
finance the expensive building on the more powerful
color group (for example, Light Blues and Yellows, or
Oranges and Greens). Your goal is to make maximum
use of the profit-earning power of each color group you
own, by exploiting one fully (at the critical level) before
beginning to work on the second. Combining a cheap
color group and an expensive color group can give you
added flexibility. In a housing shortage, you will be able
to release the necessary houses onto the housing market
by building up to hotels on your cheaper color group.
It sounds great, right? But there are two weaknesses
to the Brute Force Battle. First, it is often quite difficult
to acquire two color groups from your opponents, and
the strategy is less effective with only one color group.
Second, there is a tremendous amount of luck involved.
One bad land on an opponent's color group can ruin
your entire game. In this strategy, your opponent will
quickly realize that unless he builds to the critical level
too, he will be wiped out. He will usually copy your correct building pattern. In any fight which depends only
on slugging power, someone can land a lucky punch and
break your jaw! Although your skill and knowledge will
always give you an edge in this strategy (maybe he'll fall
into the hotel trap!), this is not enough for most tourna-

ment players. The smart guys never want to fight unless the odds are heavily stacked in their favor.

THE LYING-LOW LARCENY (the Divide-and-Conquer Strategy). This strategy is the most complicated, the most challenging, and probably the most enjoyable of the four strategies. The theme of this strategy is for you to keep your opponents at each other's throats, while you clean up quietly. Technically, a good player is always doing this (see Chapter 11), regardless of which strategy he is using, but in many situations it is a perfectly legitimate strategy all by itself. When employing the Lying-Low Larceny as your key to victory, the secret is to never appear powerful and to mislead your opponents about the true power of your position. In this strategy:

a. Build only to the critical level on a color group no more expensive than the Oranges.

b. Keep quiet about how much money you have, unless your opponents ask.

c. Do everything you can to keep other players from trading.

d. Play down the importance of your own position, pointing to those players who have more expensive color groups.

e. Quietly amass enough property, in small maneuvers which do not attract attention, to suddenly build up your properties and crush your opponents before they know what hit them.

While other chapters will explain in more detail how to carry out those strategies that you plan to undertake, this chapter should have given you a good theoretical base from which to play an intelligent, winning game. Although it is possible to win many games by using tricks and legal loopholes, you will find it much more satisfying to win game after game by simply outplaying your opponents. If you have a thorough understanding of these principles of strategy and you practice them, such satisfying victories will be yours.

CHAPTER 6 SUMMARY

    I. A strategy is good only while the conditions remain constant.

   II. Property acquisition—through bankruptcy and in lieu of rent.

 III. Strategy as a compromise.

 IV. Aim your strategies toward goals which give immediate aid.

   V. When to abandon ship.

 VI. When strategy decisions are most often made.

VII. Common strategies:

    A. Quick Kayo.

    B. Housing Hoard.

    C. Brute Force Battle.

    D. Lying-Low Larceny.

Buy and Sell What You Don't Own (Yet!)

Notwithstanding the tricks of the game, the strategic principles, and the occasional little-known rules, Monopoly is still governed to a measurable extent by the dice. On any given turn, a player may or may not land on your properties. When he does land, it is not your "skill" that caused him to roll a seven or whatever; it is your skill that caused you to prepare for that event by building houses. The skillful player is patient, for he knows that the dice will only help him in the long run. He has traded shrewdly, has developed his properties correctly, and is prepared as best he can be for sudden financial setbacks. The long-term odds are heavily in his favor. But what of the short-term odds? Can a player make the dice work for him on a turn-to-turn basis?

As was pointed out earlier, the crucial rolls of the dice are those in the first several trips around the board. In a normal four-player game, more than 75% of the properties have been bought by the time each token has passed Go five times. It would appear that during this "developmental buying period," even the skillful player has to sit back and work with whatever the dice give him. *But an alternative does exist.*

Suppose that during the buying period you manage through the luck of the dice to land on and buy two Orange properties before anyone buys the third one. You want that third Orange property pretty badly, but the odds seem stacked against you. After all, there are three other players who would love to get their hands on that property, and there is only one of you! That gives you only a 1-in-4, or 25%, chance of being the first one to land on the important Orange property. At the moment, the dice are working against you.

Let's pause for a moment to examine an analogous situation. Suppose you're betting on horses and there is a four-horse race. The first horse to cross the finish line is the winner. In this race, a correct bet will bring you the third Orange property. Why bet on only one horse (your own token) to win? Why not improve your chances at getting that prize by betting on another horse at the same time? In that case, if either horse that you bet on wins (it really doesn't matter which one), then you have won your prize. Your chances of winning have doubled, from 1-in-4 to 2-in-4! The odds are no longer against you.

You say that this is a Monopoly game and not a horse race? Well, you've got some good news coming to you—the same principle of doubling your chances of success by betting on two horses applies to Monopoly. It takes the form of an "option."

An option agreement works this way:

1. You pay another player a fixed amount of money and receive from him his option on a specified property.

2. If that player lands on that property while it is still unowned, he must purchase it and give it to you immediately, free of charge.

3. If any other player purchases the specified property first, the player who sold you his option may keep the money anyway, and has, no further obligation to you.

In our example, you could pay one of the other players $500 for his option on the third Orange property. If he agrees, then your chances of completing the Orange color group have doubled. You now have a 50–50 chance (2-in-4) of beating your opponents in the race to land on that property first. If you could buy another player's option at the same time, your chances would increase to 3-in-4, or 75%! By using your money and negotiating skill to purchase options, it is possible for you to actually turn the odds around and make them *favor* you.

* * *

Here is the way a sample option deal for New York Avenue, between Mr. Expert and Lisa Lucky, might sound:

MR. EXPERT: I would sure like to get my hands on New York Avenue, but my chances of getting it right now are pretty small. Lisa, how would you like to sell me New York Avenue?

LISA LUCKY: I'd love to, but I don't own it—it's still owned by the Bank.

MR. EXPERT: Frankly, Lisa, I don't really care whether or not you own it yet. I'd just like to buy an option on that property from you.

LISA LUCKY: Option? I've read the rules several times, and I never noticed anything about an option. What are you talking about?

MR. EXPERT: It's simple. The rules say that you can sell an unimproved property in a private transaction for any amount you can get. Since you don't own the property right now, all I want to buy from you is your promise that if you're lucky enough to land on New York Avenue, you will give it to me.

LISA LUCKY: Let me get this straight. You have no idea of whether or not I will land there first, yet you're willing to pay me money now on the possibility that I might get lucky?

MR. EXPERT: Sure. It helps me too. It increases my chance of getting the property I want. I'll give you $500 for your option on New York Avenue.

LISA LUCKY: It sounds okay to me, but what happens if you or somebody else lands on New York Avenue before I do? Do I still get to keep the money?

MR. EXPERT: You get to keep the money in any case. All you promise is that if you land there first, you will buy it with your own money and hand it over to me no questions asked.

LISA LUCKY: I think you're crazy, but I can use the $500 and my chances of landing on New York Avenue are pretty slim. It's a deal.

MR. EXPERT: We'll write the whole thing down on the back of this $1 bill, so there will be no confusion later.

The final agreement looks like the sample shown.

> I agree that if I land on N.Y. while it is still unowned, I will buy it with my own money and give it to Mr. Expert, free of charge.
>
> *Lisa Lucky*

Most of the time, you will have little trouble explaining to other players how options work. They're simple to use, and they make the "buying period" much more exciting. Be sure to stress that the player must pay for the property with his own money if he lands on it, and that this is included in the amount of money you pay him to buy his option. Once in a while, you might run up against some resistance to option agreements. Usually it will be from a third player who realizes that you are subtly increasing your chances to complete a color group. You can explain things to him very simply in the following manner:

HAMPERING HARVEY: Wait a second, not so fast. What's with all this option stuff? I read the rules and they don't say a word about any option business.
MR. EXPERT: Sure they do. Read this! *(He hands Harvey a copy of the official rules.)*
HAMPERING HARVEY: "Unimproved properties, Railroads, and utilities (but not buildings) may be sold to any player as a private arrangement, for any

amount that the owner can get." Show me where it says O-P-T-I-O-N in there.

MR. EXPERT: I'm only doing what the rules say. What I want to call it really doesn't matter. Lisa Lucky is selling me New York Avenue (an unimproved property) as a private arrangement, for any amount she can get ($500)!

HAMPERING HARVEY: But how can she sell it if she doesn't own it yet?

MR. EXPERT: If she lands on it and buys it, then she owns it! That makes her the owner. Once she becomes the owner, then she has sold me the property, in accordance with the rules. If she doesn't land on it, then she obviously can't sell me the property, and I'm out of luck. I'm paying my money on the chance that she will become the owner and we can complete the sale. I'll make the same deal with you as soon as I have the money.

HAMPERING HARVEY: Then aren't you just loaning her some money?

MR. EXPERT: Not at all. I have no intention of ever getting that money back. I am *buying* her promise to sell me the property—that's no loan.

HAMPERING HARVEY: Pretty clever! In fact, I think I'll try it myself sometime.

You are now ready to use options in your play. Before you get carried away, however, here are some important tips to remember about the strategy of option agreements:

1. Always make it clear that the player who is selling his option will be responsible for buying the property if he lands on it.

2. In general, do not buy an option unless it will complete a color group for you. There is one major exception to this principle. When your opponent is about to buy an option, remember the true value principle. If a property is very valuable to him, it is automatically valuable to you. If someone owes you a large rent, you might be able to negotiate to accept a smaller rent, with him making up the difference by giving you his option on a property which another opponent wants desperately. Think defensively, as well as offensively. The player who owes you the rent probably won't care who gets the third property, as long as it isn't the guy with the other two. He will probably sell you the option cheap, neglecting the tremendous trading value of that third property.

3. *Always put the option in writing.* Scribble the agreement on the back of a $1 bill or some other handy piece of paper. It will save you arguments later.

4. *All option agreements are* private arrangements *between two players.* If one player of the arrangement goes bankrupt, his creditor is not entitled to the option. To be safe, all options should have the name of the person who is receiving the property written on them.

5. *It is good psychological strategy to complain loudly if the option you bought fails to materialize because another player lands on the specified property first.* You paid your money, so get your money's worth in complaining. If someone made a big fuss when you originally bought the option, show him that it was all for nothing. If you land on the property first, loudly lament that all the money you spent was wasted, since you didn't need the option to get the property. If you emphasize your failures, fewer players will object to options, and they may even think that you're a sucker for buying them. Lastly, *never* gloat when your options work and you win the game.

6. *Use options to help balance the two sides of a trade.* When you and another player can't quite get together on the terms of a trade, a few well-placed options can even things out beautifully.

7. *Do not overuse options or rely on them too heavily.* They are powerful weapons when used correctly, but are also easily abused. Remember, the only time that an option guarantees that you will get a property is the time you have an option from every other player in the game. Even in that case (which is very, very rare), you still do not own the optioned property until someone lands on it. That might not be for an entire game!

8. An option is never more valuable than the property itself would be if you owned it already. If you own two Yellow properties, it is obvious that an option on the third Yellow property would be valuable. However, if there is a building shortage and you would have no houses to put on the Yellow group, the value of three Yellow properties is severely diminished. Do not think that a color group will be magically transformed into an invincible weapon, only because it was completed by a shrewd option agreement. The rules of investment analysis apply to every color group. The incorrect color group for *your* circumstances is often little better than no color group at all. An option is no better than the color group it completes.

So much for the option agreement. The next chapter deals with a similar concept. Just as an option can increase your chances of doing well and decrease the danger of bad luck, a form of "insurance" in Monopoly can do the same thing under different circumstances.

Read on! The fun is just beginning!

CHAPTER 7 SUMMARY

  I. Option agreements.
 II. Options as private agreements to sell, once you become an owner.
III. Who pays for an optioned property?
 IV. Fussing over option failure.
  V. Limits on the value of an option.

How to Stay at the Best Hotels — Free of Charge!

Now you've done it! You have just landed on Illinois Avenue with a hotel on it. It wouldn't be so bad if it weren't your opponent's hotel. To make matters worse, you don't have nearly enough money to pay the stiff $1100 rent. All of your opponents are greedily eyeing your nine little houses on the Yellow group, knowing that you'll have to tear them down to pay the debt. Things are really looking bad, and your opponent doesn't even smile when you offer him your American Express card. "You should've bought some insurance," he cracks as you glumly sell all your hard-earned houses back to the Bank for half price.

Can you buy insurance in a Monopoly game? The need is certainly there—you are constantly being exposed to the dangers of your opponents' hotels. Of course, there is no insurance company selling policies, but then you don't really need a company to buy insurance. Other games have forms of insurance. Look at the game of Blackjack (Twenty-one). If you're playing in a casino in Las Vegas and the dealer shows an ace up, he'll always ask the bettors if they want to buy "insurance." A player may then bet on whether or not the dealer has a picture card or a ten-spot face down (which would give him Blackjack). If he does have one, the insurance buyers are paid off and the dealer collects all other bets; if not, those who bought insurance lose what they paid and the game goes on as if nothing had happened. Players who buy insurance feel that it is better to be safe than sorry, while players who pass up the opportunity decide to take their chances. The same can be done in Monopoly.

There are three types of "insurance" that are commonly bought and sold during a Monopoly game. The only difference between these types is the duration of the insurance policy coverage. Everyone knows the maxim that "time is money," and this is especially true in the insurance business. The longer you want your coverage to last, the more it is going to cost you. Here is a brief explanation of the three types of insurance which are used.

The simplest and briefest type of policy is the "free pass." Suppose we examine the situation of Bad Luck Bobbie, who just landed on Illinois Avenue and owes $1100 to the owner of the Red group, Rita. On the previous turn, Bobbie was sitting on St. James Place, right in front of the disastrous Reds. When it became his turn to roll the dice, he studied the board for a moment and quickly noted that he needed to roll anything but a five, seven, or eight. Now, Bobbie's no mathematician, but he knows that five, seven, and eight are pretty common numbers, no matter how hard he prays for them to go away. If any one of those common numbers turn up on the dice, he'll be on Rita's Red group with a lot of money to pay. What's a mother to do?

We already know that Bobbie is destined to land on Illinois Avenue and we can't alter fate, so we suggest to our unfortunate friend that he ask to buy a free pass. He could say something like:

"Listen, Rita. We both know that I'm in perfect position to land on your hotels. However, we also know that my chances of missing them are pretty good, too. *(In fact, they're almost 6-in-10, Bobbie!)* How does this sound? I'll give you $300 now, and no matter what happens on my next turn, I'll be all paid up. If I don't land on one of your properties, the cash is still yours to keep. If I do . . . that's why I bought the free pass! If you take the cash now, you're sure of some money, and

$300 is nothing to sneeze at. Don't worry, I'll be coming around the board again soon enough, so you'll have plenty of shots at me again."

As things turned out, this would have been a good deal for Bobbie. This one-shot insurance would have saved him $800 from the cost of the rent on Illinois Avenue. Had he known enough to make the offer, he could have saved himself a lot of heartache.

The free pass idea can also have many variations. A wild possibility could have the owner of the Dark Blue group selling insurance against drawing the infamous "Advance to Boardwalk" card. An insured player who draws that card would not have to pay the rent on Boardwalk when he draws it. This type of free pass would normally sell for about $400.

The next type of insurance that is commonly bought and sold is slightly more durable than the free pass. In the previous chapter, you learned of the option agreement. Its insurance counterpart is the "prepayment option," more commonly referred to as a "free land." Let's go back to Bobbie, who is sitting dejectedly on Illinois Avenue. He managed to save his houses on the Yellows, but he had to give up two key properties to raise the money. Bobbie now knows enough to constantly plan ahead. While his opponents are building up their color groups, he decides to make the following offer to Happy Hope, owner of the Oranges:

"Hope, how would you like to earn a quick $250? You could use it, since you don't have much cash at the moment, and it would certainly come in handy if you landed on somebody else's color group. If you take the offer I'm about to make, you won't have to sell those nice houses on your Oranges back to the Bank for half price if you need money. Right now, I'm nowhere near your Oranges, but I'd like to buy a free land on them as a sort of insurance. I'll give you the $250 immediately if you let me land there free, just once. The only condition is that I get to pick when to use my free land."

Bobbie is asking for more than just a free pass for one turn. This free land is not "spent" until Bobbie has actually used it by landing rent-free on the Oranges. Depending on the situation, this can be a good deal for both players. Free lands make the future less dangerous and are a powerful device for buying time. With a promise of one or more free lands on one or more of your opponents' color groups, you can be protected against sudden expensive rents in the near future. Not only will you sleep better at night, but you will also be freer to invest heavily in your own color groups. You will no longer need to keep that cash cushion against financial reverses which could force you to sell houses at a loss.

It can also be a very wise move to sell free lands. The player who needs cash to avoid selling a couple of expensive houses is usually playing wisely if he sells a free land instead of selling the houses. Even if a player is not in serious debt, selling a free land can be a good way to raise cash to build more houses. Although he will owe one of his opponents a free land, he will be able to offset the lost income by investing right away and collecting even higher rents from the other players.

There are dozens of ways that an imaginative player can utilize free lands. For example,

a. He can trade free lands. "I'll give you one on the Red group if you give me one on the Yellows."

b. He can pay all or part of a rent with free lands. "I owe you $750. I'll give you a free land on the Dark Blues and $200, and we can call it even."

c. He can use free lands as part of a trade. "If I give you the Red group and I get only the Orange group, then I want two free lands on those Reds to make up for the difference in rents."

d. He can sell free lands on one property out of an entire color group. "I'll sell you a free land on Park Place, but not on Boardwalk."

The ways in which free lands can be employed are limitless. They can be a tremendous addition to the skill and excitement of any Monopoly game. But be careful! There are several tricks to watch out for in any game in which free lands are sold. A knowledgeable player is aware of all of them:

1. Be sure that any agreement involving free lands makes it clear *at whose discretion the free lands will be used up*. For example, suppose you buy a free land on an opponent's Red group, and by the time you land on that color group, there are no houses standing on it. Must you take the free land right then and there (and use it up), or can you save it and use it when your free land will be more valuable to you? If this wasn't settled at the time of the free land sale, you will find yourself in the middle of a large fight. The owner of the Red group is sure to insist that it's your tough luck—your free land is now used up. On the other hand, this is obviously unacceptable to you. The only way to resolve such a conflict is to prevent it altogether. Whenever you make a trade involving free lands, make it clear to your opponent that either (*a*) the free lands will be used up each time the recipient of them lands on the properties or (*b*) the free lands may be used whenever the recipient decides to use them.

If you don't put the agreement in writing, make sure that all the other players in the game hear and remember at whose discretion the free lands are to be taken.

2. The next, finer point concerns the "transferability" of free lands. Suppose that Rita has sold Jerry five free lands on her Red group. Suppose also that Bad Luck Bobbie has done it again, and landed on Illinois Avenue one more time. Bobbie hasn't bought any free lands from Rita and isn't too happy about owing Rita another $1100. But now Jerry speaks up. The dialogue goes like this:

JERRY: Bobbie, things might not be as bad as they seem. I have five free lands on Rita's Reds, and I certainly don't need all of them. How about if I sell you one of them right now for $500, and then you will have saved yourself $600 *($1100 − 500 = 600)*

RITA: Wait a second, here. You can't do that. I sold

you those free lands, Jerry. You can't go around giving them away to whomever you please. I sold them to you as a *private arrangement* between the two of us. That agreement applies only to the times that *you* land on my properties.

Rita is right. Just as it is illegal to transfer options, either by sale or through bankruptcy, so it is illegal to transfer free lands, by sale or through bankruptcy. The power to make private agreements resides solely in the ownership of a property—it does not float around with agreements such as options or free lands.

Be certain to make this fact clear whenever you sell someone a free land on your property. To be completely safe, it is best to write the agreement down and to specify that this is a "nontransferable" free land which you are selling.

3. The third pitfall which becomes evident in dealing with free lands is extremely important, not only with regard to free lands themselves, but for its implications regarding many other types of trades. Consider the following situation. Gary owns the Green group and Rita owns the Red group. Gary and Rita decide to trade each other one free land on their color groups. Gray gives Rita a $1 bill with the conditions written on the back, and Rita does likewise. But Gary is a sneaky sort of a guy, and he decides to sell his Green group to his friend Kathy. Kathy wastes no time in developing her new Green group, building plenty of houses. Soon enough, the investment begins to pay off. Rita lands on Pacific Avenue with three houses built on it and owes Kathy $900 rent. Rita tries to use the free land on the Greens which she got from Gary. *But she can't!* That free land is no longer valid, since the free land was *a promise by Gary and the rent is owed to Kathy!* Rita is furious. She never got a chance to use her free land!

In revenge, she turns to Gary and exclaims, "Since I never got to use my free land on your Greens, you can't use the free land I gave you on my Reds!" But Gary is no fool. He quietly explains to Rita that she can't suddenly refuse to honor her promise of a free land, as long as she still owns the Reds, just as he could not refuse to honor the free land he had given her, as long as he owned the Greens.

There are two important rules demonstrated in this situation:

A PROMISE TO GRANT ANOTHER PLAYER A PRIVILEGE REGARDING A COLOR GROUP IS A PERSONAL ARRANGEMENT AND DOES NOT BECOME IN ANY WAY "ATTACHED" TO THE PROPERTIES THEMSELVES. SUCH PROMISES ARE ENFORCEABLE ONLY AGAINST THE PLAYER WHO MADE THE PROMISE.

In other words, whenever a property is traded, all promises made concerning that property are nullified. In addition:

WHEN SUCH PROMISES ARE NULLIFIED BY A PROPERTY TRANSFER, ANY PROMISES MADE CONCERNING OTHER PROPERTIES ARE STILL ENFORCEABLE, EVEN IF THOSE PROMISES WERE PART OF THE SAME TRADE IN WHICH THE NULLIFIED PROMISES WERE FIRST MADE.

This is just a specific case of the general rule that *no promise may be withdrawn unilaterally.**

So don't get caught like Rita did! Understand all the ramifications of every free land agreement which you make.

We have now covered the first two types of insurance. The free pass lets a player go by a color group once, and is gone after the next turn, whether or not the player ac-

---

* It is possible to construct very complicated arrangements which would cancel all promises made in a trade if any one of those promises was ever nullified, but such arrangements add an unnecessary complication to the theory of free lands. The reason such arrangements are so complicated is that they must always obey the principles of *never violating the rules* and *never restricting the rights of property owners which are specified in the rules.* For the purposes of this book, all promises of immunity will follow the more popular and simpler guidelines given above.

tually *lands* on the color group. The free land actually lets a player *land* rent-free on his opponent's property. Now, we come to the use of "total immunity."

Total immunity is the logical final extension of the concept of insurance. Granting or selling a player total immunity guarantees that for as long as you own the properties, the player who receives immunity will never have to pay any rent on them. Immunity is a private arrangement of the most powerful type, often lasting the entire duration of a game. However, the knowledgeable player understands that immunity, like free lands, is only a private arrangement and is in no way tied to the properties themselves. It is vital to realize that any promise of immunity or a color group is destroyed if that color group is traded, sold, or transferred by bankruptcy. Consequently, several of the tricks described earlier with regard to free lands are just as applicable to immunity. The power to grant immunity, like free lands, is a right of the owner and is therefore nontransferable. This should be made clear any time you grant immunity.

Why would any player give total immunity on his color groups and thus deprive himself of a source of rent for the rest of the game? Here are several possible reasons:

THE DETENTE IMMUNITY STRATEGY. You can give immunity to get immunity. It's the old idea of "I won't hurt you if you won't hurt me." It can be very valuable to neutralize a strong opponent while you gobble up the smaller fish in the sea. Then, when you are ready to take on the big one, you will have new weapons with which to end your detente.

THE TRADER VIC IMMUNITY STRATEGY. You can give immunity to get something very valuable. "If you give me the third Light Blue property, allowing me to complete the Light Blue group, I will give you total immunity on my Red group. Instead of paying me $1000, you'll be paying me a lot less." You can use this powerful argument in order to have the rest of your opponents paying on two color groups instead of one.

THE SAVE YOUR SKIN IMMUNITY STRATEGY. You can give immunity because you're desperate for cash. "I know I owe you $1000, but I'm willing to give you three free lands on my Yellows if you'll call it off. No, eh? Okay, I'll give you total immunity on my Yellows!"

THE TEMPTING CANDY IMMUNITY STRATEGY. You can use immunity as a lure to trick your opponent. Once you have given your opponent immunity and he has given you whatever it is that you wanted, you can trade your color group away and destroy his immunity. Admittedly, this is rather ruthless and it might upset him at the time, but don't worry—he'll try to do the same thing to you next game.

Immunity is a very enticing promise to offer another player or to receive yourself. Be extremely careful when making trades which include immunity. If you are playing with opponents who have never seen it before, you are at a tremendous advantage. If, on the other hand, your opponents have learned the concept and understand the possible tricks associated with it, you must be much more careful. Immunity alters the entire balance of power in a Monopoly game and affects everything, from investment analysis to strategy selection. It should be offered only when appropriate—keep in mind that in many cases free lands will satisfy a player just as well.

How do we justify the concepts of free passes, free lands, and immunity in light of the official rules? It's simple! The rules, either intentionally or unwittingly, have made it perfectly legal for one player not to pay rent on another player's property when he lands there. The rule is as follows: *The owner may not collect his rent if he fails to ask for it before the second player following throws the dice.*

The key word in this rule is "fails." The rule does not say "if he *forgets* to ask for it," so the fact that the owner is aware that he is failing to collect the rent is completely irrelevant. Even if other players in the game remind him that he may collect the rent, he may still "fail to ask for it." The decision of whether or not to fail to ask for rent is *completely at the discretion of the owner* and cannot be influenced by the other players.

From here, it is a short jump to the concepts of free passes, free lands, and immunity. Simply combine the rule making any sale a "private arrangement" with the previous rule, and you have the perfectly legal opportunity to make a "private arrangement" to "fail to ask" for the rent, under conditions agreed upon by both players. A free pass is a private arrangement to fail to ask for the rent if the player lands on a specific color group on his next turn. A free land is a private arrangement to fail to ask for the rent for a specific number of lands on a color group. Immunity is a private arrangement to fail to ask for the rent for the rest of the time that the player who is making the promise owns those properties.

Easy!

In the following chapters, the concepts of free passes, free lands, and immunity will all be shown to be only a part of the tremendous arsenal of trading weapons. The skilled player uses them all, along with his imagination, to heighten the excitement of the game and to ensure victory over less skillful opponents.

CHAPTER 8 SUMMARY

    I. Insurance.
   II. Free passes—one-shot insurance.
 III. Free lands—guaranteed collection.
 IV. Free lands at whose discretion?
   V. Transferability of free lands.
 VI. Free lands destroyed by property transfer.

VII. Immunity.
VIII. Immunity strategies:
    A. Detente.
    B. Trader Vic.
    C. Save-Your-skin.
    D. Tempting Candy.
IX. Immunity as a "private arrangement" to "fail to ask."

Pick Your Partner, Dough-C-Dough

"One, two, three, four, five . . . Park Place? It's unowned! I'll buy it. Now all I need is Boardwalk and I'll have myself a complete color group." We all say something like this during every game we play. If it's not about Boardwalk and Park Place, then maybe we have two Orange properties and need the third one. We were lucky enough to get two properties—why shouldn't we be just as lucky and get the third?

Don't hold your breath. The chances are, only once in every 11 games will you be the first player to land on every property in a three-property color group. For the two-property color groups, you will be the first one to land on both properties about once in every eight games (and one of those groups is the Purples!). It looks as if you'd better find something other than your luck to pull you through.

Well, suppose you try a trick that you now have up your sleeve. You own Park Place and you want Boardwalk, so the thing to do is to increase your chances of getting Boardwalk by buying one or two other players' options on Boardwalk. You discreetly ask one of your opponents for what price he would sell his option on Boardwalk. He smiles and replies, "$1000."

"A thousand dollars," you scream. "That's outrageous!" Meanwhile, the other players quickly agree that they would never sell their options for less than $1000. It looks like your opponents are putting a squeeze on, so options are out of the question for the time being. But you are not beaten so easily, so you sit back and wait patiently.

It doesn't take long for disaster to strike. Not only does someone land on Boardwalk before you do, but it's none other than Cathy Cautious, the last person in the world you wanted to have to deal with. Cathy Cautious is always "out to lunch," if you know what we mean. She likes Boardwalk because of the nice $50 rent and sees no reason to do anything but relax and contentedly collect $50 every time someone lands there. This could pose a pretty tough trading problem!

Here's how Mr. Expert would handle things. His first step is to make a few tentative propositions:

MR. EXPERT: Cathy? . . . CATHY?

CATHY CAUTIOUS: Wait a minute, I'm counting my $1 bills. I'm almost finished . . . There, I'm done.

MR. EXPERT: How would you like to sell me your Boardwalk?

CATHY CAUTIOUS: Not really.

MR. EXPERT: Perhaps you'd like to trade it for one of my properties. I own a lot of nice properties.

CATHY CAUTIOUS: Do you have any properties with bigger rents?

MR. EXPERT: Well, I could give you my three Railroads. They have a rent of $100!

CATHY CAUTIOUS: No, I can't build houses on the Railroads. Besides, why should I trade Boardwalk? It's the best property on the board! Look, with a hotel I can get $2000!

MR. EXPERT: That's true, but you can't build a hotel unless you also own Park Place, and at the moment I have Park Place.

CATHY CAUTIOUS: Oh. Well, I guess $50 is plenty for me.

MR. EXPERT: Wouldn't you rather collect $2000?

CATHY CAUTIOUS: But you just said I couldn't unless I owned Park Place too, and you own Park Place.

MR. EXPERT: Maybe we can make some sort of a deal where we can both do very well.

CATHY CAUTIOUS: I don't know about your "deals." Let me hear about it first.

Assuming you've done as well as Mr. Expert has so far, you're still going to have to come up with a pretty good deal to convince "out-to-lunch" Cathy to part with her treasured Boardwalk. Here's one idea that might work:

You remember that in an option agreement one player gives up cash now for the promise of a property later. Why not turn that idea around to fit your present circumstances? Instead of giving *cash now* for *property later,* why not find a way for a player to give *property now* for *cash later?*

The way is called "revenue sharing." It works this way:

1. One player contributes property to complete another player's color group. By completing the color group, the other player can begin building and collecting 10–100 times what he was collecting before.

2. As compensation for receiving the property, the new owner of the color group promises the player who contributed the property that he will pay him a percentage of all cash revenues (rent money) which he ever collects on that color group. A standard percentage to give to the player who surrenders his property is 50%.

Let's see how Mr. Expert would use the concept of revenue sharing to make a trade with Cathy:

MR. EXPERT: How does this deal sound, Cathy? If you give me Boardwalk, I'll build houses on the complete color group and give *you* half of any money I collect there.

CATHY CAUTIOUS: You want me to *give* you Boardwalk?

MR. EXPERT: You are not *giving* me anything, we are combining together. You let me hold the properties and we'll split the profits. In just a short while, we'll be rolling in dough. The combination will help both of us.

CATHY CAUTIOUS: If it will help us both so much, why don't you give me Park Place? After all, I have the expensive property and you have the cheaper one.

MR. EXPERT: Listen, Cathy, it's not important who has the expensive property and who has the cheap one. The important thing is that I have lots of cash to buy houses with, and you don't.

CATHY CAUTIOUS: If I give you Boardwalk, you'll be spending *your* money to build houses, not mine?

MR. EXPERT: That's right. I'll spend my own money to pay for the buildings, but I'll give you half of any money I collect.

CATHY CAUTIOUS: But suppose I land on them myself. Do I have to pay you?

MR. EXPERT: I'll give you immunity too. You will *never* have to pay as long as I own those properties.

CATHY CAUTIOUS: Let me get this straight: I give you Boardwalk, you build houses on the color group out of your own money, and I get half the money you collect on *either* Boardwalk *or* Park Place. On top of that, I never have to pay you rent on Boardwalk or Park Place if I land on them. Is that your offer?

MR. EXPERT: That's it. The more I build, the more money I collect. The more money I collect, the more profits we can split. We both benefit!

CATHY CAUTIOUS: I'll take that trade any day of the week! I give up only one property, and in return I get immunity and a promise of a lot more money in the future.

MR. EXPERT: So it's a deal then?

CATHY CAUTIOUS: It's a deal!

Welcome to the world of partnerships! Not partnerships in the real-world sense, where there would be two owners of the same property (that's illegal under the rules), but Monopoly game partnerships. Why call it a partnership if there aren't two owners? We refer to it as a partnership because both players continue to have an interest in the color group, even after the first part of the transaction is completed.

A Monopoly game partnership is defined as any

agreement in which one player gives property to complete another player's color group and in return receives a promise of immunity and some percentage of revenue sharing. Other considerations might be given, but any time there is both immunity and revenue sharing, a partnership has been formed. The person who owns the properties can be thought of as the landlord of the buildings. The other player can be thought of as an investor (he invested his property). Although the landlord is the person who actually collects the rent money, he owes a portion of his rent to the investor. The result is a private arrangement between the investor and the landlord.

Partnerships can make things a little more complicated and a lot trickier. Unless you know the ins and outs of private arrangements, partnership agreements can be full of dangerous traps. But don't be alarmed. A player who *does* know what he's doing and knows how to convince other players to form partnerships has a tremendous edge, an almost unbeatable edge. A player who isn't familiar with partnerships is no match for one who is. Let's examine some of the specific strategies that the skilled partnership architect uses:

A PARTNERSHIP IS A PRIVATE ARRANGEMENT, JUST AS OPTIONS, FREE PASSES, FREE LANDS, AND IMMUNITY ARE PRIVATE ARRANGEMENTS. As such, it has all the inherent advantages and disadvantages of any private arrangement. If you own the Yellows and have promised Peter Partner half of the rents you collect, Peter is no longer entitled to collect half the rents from the *new* owner if you trade those Yellows away. A partnership agreement is very fragile.

THE OWNER OF A COLOR GROUP, EVEN IF HE HAS PROMISED HALF THE RENTS TO A PARTNER, IS STILL THE SOLE OWNER OF THAT COLOR GROUP. None of his rights of property ownership are altered in any way from those established in the rules. His partner may make no decisions concerning the administration of the property. For instance, the partner may not buy or sell houses, mortgage the property, or sell it to another player. He is like a bondholder in a company. He gets his money, but he makes no direct contribution to the actual day-to-day operations of the corporation. All he can do is collect his money and give advice if it is requested.

THE OWNER OF THE COLOR GROUP HAS TREMENDOUS ADVANTAGES OVER HIS PARTNER. The importance of ownership should never be underestimated. By forming even one early partnership in which you are the owner, you can win the game. Why all the emphasis on being the owner and not the partner? Let's re-examine the entire partnership arrangement, this time with the tools of investment analysis.

Going back to our last example, we see that Mr. Expert now owns Boardwalk and Park Place. At first glance, the inexperienced player would say that Cathy Cautious did pretty well for herself. After all, Mr. Expert does have to pay for all the houses with his own money, and the critical level is pretty expensive to reach on the Dark Blue group (6 × $200 per house = $1200). And then he still pays Cathy half of whatever money he collects from rent! It doesn't look like Mr. Expert was so smart after all. But let's look even closer.

Mr. Expert has, in fact, kept three out of the four advantages of owning a color group completely within his control! Here are the four advantages and the way they were affected by the formation of the partnership:

1. Bankrupting power. As owner of the Dark Blues, Mr. Expert retains all the bankrupting power of the color group. When he only owned Park Place, he had no bankrupting power whatsoever. Now, even though he has a partner, he is the owner of a powerful color group which is easily capable of bankrupting other players.

*   *   *

QUESTION: What happens if Mr. Expert bankrupts another player and obtains all of the bankrupt player's properties? Is he obliged to give half of them to
Cathy?

ANSWER: *No!* Mr. Expert agreed to divide the *cash*
rents he collected, and no more. It is also obviously
impossible to tear a property in half, even if he
wanted to.

In most partnership trades, this tremendous advantage for the owner is overlooked. If the question arises,
the owner should explain that his ability to drive another
player into bankruptcy is fair compensation for all of his
expensive investments in buildings. A shrewd player will
try to minimize the importance of the bankrupting power
by pointing out how far away everyone is from bankruptcy, all the while remembering how important the
power to bankrupt is to any winning strategy.

2. *House-soaking power.* Mr. Expert, as the owner of
the Dark Blues, has sole control over when houses get
built and when they get torn down. Although the Dark
Blues are not very efficient for soaking up houses, they
are useful in bidding for houses during a housing shortage, and whatever house-soaking power the color group
possesses, it is certainly under Mr. Expert's control. It is
also possible to form a partnership on the Light Blue
group, for instance, in which case the owner would have
an even more significant house-soaking and house-re-
leasing advantage.

3. *Glamour power.* If Mr. Expert ever decides that
paying Cathy half of all the rents he collects is no longer
profitable, he can always trade the color group away. It
would cost him some money, as he would have to sell
expensive houses back to the Bank for half price (no
color group may be traded while houses are still standing on it), but Mr. Expert could work that cost into the
trade. If he were to decide to trade the Dark Blues to
another player, there would be nothing that Cathy Cautious could do except become very angry. The owner of
a property can trade or sell that property at any time

during the game, to whomever he wishes. In a partnership, the owner does not suffer nearly as much from the trade of the color group as the partner does. While the owner gets compensation from this second trade, his partner ends up with nothing. There is little that Cathy can do if Mr. Expert wants to use the glamour of the Dark Blues as bait in a trade.

4. *Profit-earning power.* Where actual cash revenues are concerned, Mr. Expert has given up half of all the rents he collects, and Cathy is on an equal footing. This is a small price to pay, considering all the other advantages which Mr. Expert has acquired. But there is still another advantage which becomes especially significant in this situation: *the owner of a property has the power to decide whether or not, and in what form, he collects the rent owed to him.* Mr. Expert only agreed to pay Cathy "half the cash revenues which he collects." (If he was careful, he put the whole thing in writing.) That leaves a good deal of leeway for some financial maneuvering with the profit-earning power of his color group. For example, he could accept property, options, free lands, or any such item instead of payment, whenever his opponents land on the Dark Blues.

QUESTION: If Mr. Expert was supposed to collect $1100, but instead accepted a property, does he owe Cathy Cautious any money?

ANSWER: *No!* The agreement stated that Mr. Expert owes Cathy one half the *cash revenues collected.* If he doesn't collect any cash, he doesn't owe Cathy any.

Mr. Expert can do whatever he wishes with regard to the actual collection of rents on the color group. He may grant immunity to other players, give free lands, give free passes, or fail to ask for the rent (accidentally or on purpose), just as if he were the owner of the color group without any partner.

On all four advantages, Mr. Expert has the upper

hand. Using the strategy of partnerships, you can do the same in your games.

It's going to be a lot of fun for you to try to convince your opponents that you're offering them a fair deal when you know how advantageous that deal really is for you. You saw how convincing Mr. Expert was when he spoke to Cathy. Here are some pointers to keep in mind when you are negotiating to form a partnership:

1. Make it clear that the partnership will benefit *both* players.
2. Point out that you will be paying for all the houses that you buy. All your partner will have to do is collect the money without lifting a finger.
3. Play down the importance of the touchy advantages of ownership, should they come up. If your partner questions you on taking property instead of cash, tell him that it would be impossible for you to rip a property in half. Besides, players rarely offer property, and you need the cash anyway.
4. Stress the idea that if you can cooperate now, you and your partner could also cooperate and help each other later.
5. If your partner asks about what would happen if you bankrupt another player, explain that you would get the properties, but this is your only compensation for the costs of building. You can also explain that by the time anyone goes bankrupt, the entire game will be very different.
6. Play down the possibility that you could trade the property away and destroy everything. Agree to build houses immediately if that will reassure your partner. Use the argument, "After all, why should I mess things up if I already have a good thing going?"
7. Never antagonize your partner any earlier than is absolutely necessary. Other players will be watching to see if your deals are as fair as you say they are. If it isn't necessary to take properties instead of rent money, then don't. Paying your partner half the rent money you col-

lect builds up your reputation for fairness and your credibility with the other players. Your reputation is very important. Players will not trade with you if they see that you once turned around and hurt your partner the minute you completed a trade.

8. When it is time to explain something unfortunate to your partner, do so gently and with sympathy. Your partner is likely to get very upset when someone goes bankrupt on your color group and he gets none of the properties. Never let it appear that you tricked him into agreeing to something which he did not understand, or that you are twisting his words to take advantage of him.

9. Try to form partnerships as early as possible. This is really only another way of saying that the earlier you acquire your own color group, the better off you are.

10. Never tolerate a grabby partner. The correct procedure for collecting rents is for the rent to be first collected by the owner. *Then,* the correct percentage must be given to the partner. Don't let your partner collect "his half" straight from the debtor. The private arrangement is between you and your partner, not between the debtor and your partner. If you make sure that you are always paid the full amount first, it is very clear who is the owner and who is the partner. Your partner may *never* demand money from the player who landed on *your* color group. If the owner fails to ask for the rent, then no rent is collected—it's that simple. Your partner cannot do the asking for you, just as he cannot mortage properties in your color group.

11. Sometimes your partner will want to contribute cash to help your building effort. He might realize that the more houses that are built, the more money he will be receiving. He's correct, and you should feel fortunate that your interests coincide with his. But be careful:

a. Your partner may *not* buy the houses himself and put them on your color group. He must first transfer the cash to you by buying something (like a "Get out of Jail Free" card or the Water Works—you can always buy it back for $1 later). *You* must then buy the houses for *your* color group. This two-step process must always be respected; *no player may ever build on another player's color group*.

b. If you sell your houses, even if your opponent helped to pay for them, he does not receive any money for their sale. You should make it very clear to your partner whenever he transfers money to you for house-building that he has no financial interest in those houses. You are the owner of the color group and all improvements on them, and you may do with them as you wish. Your partner may never contribute money for houses on the condition that you will never sell those houses. This would be an illegal restriction on the rights of a property owner. If your partner objects to such rules, point out that you will be quite happy to spend your own money to buy the houses—just as soon as you can afford them.

Do not get the idea that a partnership is no more than a nasty trick which benefits only the owner, or that once your friends understand the powers of ownership, no one will ever form partnerships again. *A partnership really does benefit both players*. It just benefits the owner much more. It is quite possible (in fact, it is very common in expert play) to find compensation for the partner. This compensation can take the form of the options and/or partnerships on second and third color groups. Large minimum building requirements can reduce the danger that immunity and half profits will be nullified by a trade. Formation of a partnership with one player could also force another player to make a favorable trade with you, the partner, when he would not have been willing to make that trade before. As long as you are fully aware of the dangers involved, it is quite reasonable for you to want to form a partnership, even if you are forced to allow the other player to become the owner. Until you are fully comfortable with the theories of partnership strategy, however, it is much quicker and simpler if you can arrange to be the owner in a partnership. Don't make your life any more complicated than you have to!

The last three chapters have introduced the major offensive tactics for winning Monopoly games. Combining these tactics with the new strategy considerations to be explained in the next several chapters willl enable you to demolish any amateur. But should these not be enough, there are still plenty of unusual ploys and humorous tricks left to go. Next, we will examine the way some of the offensive weapons can be best used in light of some general trading principles and priorities.

CHAPTER 9 SUMMARY

   I. Revenue sharing—property now for cash later.
  II. Partnerships—immunity plus revenue sharing.
 III. A partnership is a private arrangement.
 IV. The owner is still sole owner.
  V. The owner has advantages.
 VI. Fine points of partnership negotiation.
VII. Partnerships really benefit both partners.

Trick or Trade

You know what to trade and you know the value of each of the various trading devices. Now comes the difficult part: the arts of *knowing when to trade* and *knowing how to "talk a trade."* Many players can do one, but not the other. A successful trader must be able to do both. One of the reasons that Monopoly games are so much fun is that they force players to combine the skills of the banker, investor, landlord, builder, and salesman. This chapter will emphasize the profession of salesman.

It has been said that a smooth salesman could sell sand to the Arabs or ice to the Eskimos. What are the characteristics of the successful salesman which are most applicable to Monopoly?

1. He knows when the mood of the game is ripe for a trade.

2. He can spot a bargain and pursue it.

3. He knows the true value of what he is buying and selling.

4. He understands his opponents and uses the appropriate form of delivering his sales pitch.

This chapter will review each of those characteristics in detail, explaining the correct application of each one to the game plan of an expert.

The first requirement of a good trader is that he *know when to speak up.* Usually, players are most receptive to trade offers if:

a. *They're in big trouble and need help,*

b. They're aggressive and want to improve their position, or

c. They have seen a prediction which you made earlier come true.

Of these three reasons, the first one is the most obvious. When a player has suddenly landed on an opponent's property with an expensive hotel, even the quietest players liven up. This is the best time to make trades, since a drowning player has little choice but to accept any lifeline thrown his way. A word of caution here: Monopoly is a game of intense pride for many players, and they would rather go bankrupt than be forced to accept a ridiculous, humiliating deal. (This attitude will be explored more thoroughly in Chapter 12.) Therefore, a good salesman trades on the best terms he can get when dealing with a player in deep trouble, taking extra care not to embarrass him or take unfair advantage of him.

A player can be in serious trouble without actually landing on an opponent's property. Many players are smart enough to see when things are about to take a turn for the worse. Instead of waiting until their backs are against the wall, they are willing to talk about protecting themselves in advance. A shrewd trader can spot such opportunities to give protection. For instance, suppose your opponent Don is approaching the Red group owned by Jeff. Throughout the game, Don has been threatening to break Jeff's arm if he doesn't tear down his hotels on the Red group. Jeff has constantly refused (after first checking to see if his Blue Cross covers damages from enraged Monopoly players*). Now, Don is sitting on the Pennsylvania Railroad, in perfect position to land on those hideous hotels which are six, eight, and nine squares away. Don has almost no cash and is jealously eyeing the $1500 sitting in front of you. He knows, being a smart trader himself, that if he waits until he lands on Jeff's hotel, he will be in a terrible position to bargain. *Nobody likes to bargain from a posi-*

---

* Most Blue Cross policies do not provide compensation for injuries resulting from war.

tion of weakness. Therefore, Don, realizing that he is in serious danger of landing on the Reds, turns to you and offers to make some sort of trade. This is a great time for you to buy Don's option on the third Light Blue property which you have been trying to get. You could probably buy the option for much less than you normally could. If you are especially sharp, you might try to buy his option on one of the properties which is crucial for another player. In any event, whenever your opponents are in trouble, or *think* they are in trouble, it is a golden trading opportunity.

The second situation which a good trader looks for is the presence of an aggressive trader. This is the guy who is always offering the worst deals at the loudest volume. Some of his standard suggestions:

"I'll give you $175 for Boardwalk . . . Too low? $200!"

"I'll trade you any one of my Railroads for that Maroon property."

"Sure I'll give you Park Place. You give me all your money and all your properties!" (This is known in tournament circles as the D.F. strategy, after a friend of ours who invented it.)

Every game has a player like this. You must be very careful not to associate your good deals with his attempted robberies. However, you can use this type of player to your advantage. The odds are good that he has no idea of the true significance of many of the ingenious offers which you can propose to him. Look at the following example where Larry Loudmouth tries to acquire the third Railroad owned by Mr. Expert.

LARRY LOUDMOUTH: Hey, Mr. Expert, I'll give you $300 for your Railroad. You paid only $200 for it—you'd make a 50% profit!

MR. EXPERT: Sure, if you also give me immunity from paying on all your Railroads and a promise to buy and give me Illinois Avenue if you ever land on it.

LARRY LOUDMOUTH: What?

MR. EXPERT: If you really want the Railroad, I'll sell it

to you for $300 if you agree that I never have to pay
rent on any of your Railroads, and if you promise to
buy Illinois Avenue and give it to me free if you ever
land on it. Don't you understand?

LARRY LOUDMOUTH: Yeah, I do. (*He hesitates, wondering if he's been outsmarted.*) Okay, that's fine.

The best way to trap an aggressive player is to catch
him at his own game. Aggressive players will rarely admit their mistakes or their ignorance. Use this opportunity to slip a few fast ones by them. The other players in
the game will probably be very happy to see Larry
Loudmouth eat his words and lick his wounds.

The third situation in which players are most receptive to trades is the trickiest one to judge. Usually, when
you have made a prediction earlier in the game and that
prediction has proved itself accurate, it is a good time to
speak up. Depending on what the other players in the
game are like, you might suggest a trade, using the tone
of, "You didn't listen to me before. Now, see what happened?" The risk here is that your opponents might not
want to be reminded that they made a mistake in not listening to you the first time. The proper approach is to
hint subtly that the last prediction was insignificant when
compared with the disaster approaching if some sort of
agreement isn't made right away. Scare tactics as this
one should be attempted only after a good deal of patience, and after all other logical approaches to set up a
trade have been exhausted. However, once in a while it
is fun to be able to pat yourself on the back and sneer at
your unyielding opponent, "I told you so!"

The second characteristic of a crack salesman is his
ability to spot a bargain. Suppose that Bob Builder
wants to raise cash so that he can build a few more
houses on his color group. As far as Bob Builder is concerned, he has only one thing to sell—his properties.
(We are assuming that he hasn't already read this book
and is not yet familiar with options, free lands, and reve-

nue sharing.) He reluctantly asks the other players in
the game if they would like to buy one or two of his
properties. At this point, one of two things can happen:

a. The vultures in the game, all thinking that they can
make a killing, quickly swoop in and try to make a fast
deal for the property of Bob's that they really need.

b. Nobody is really interested in buying Bob's properties, since either his prices are too high or his properties
aren't very valuable.

If everyone, smelling a sale, jumps at Bob's offer, you
should wait patiently until the screaming has stopped
before making your move. If it looks as if Bob is about
to make a quick sale, however, stop him. Explain that
you'll buy a property that he doesn't even own—an option. Since Bob was probably reluctant to sell his property in the first place, this should appeal to him. If there
are no options worth buying, try to undercut your opponents by offering things which they can't offer. If you
have a developed color group, offer a free land and
$200 cash for one of his juiciest properties. If Bob is in-
terested only in raising cash, use your ingenuity in combining the tactics and devices which you have learned to
make sure that he will make the trade with *you.*

If Bob's offer draws no serious bids for his property,
this is a good opportunity for you to pick up a property
very cheaply. If he needs cash, you should *not* offer to
buy a utility or a Railroad (unless you own the other
three Railroads). If you don't want to buy whatever Bob
is offering, or you have no money, this can still be the
perfect time for a counteroffer. You can be sure that
Bob will be listening and willing to trade, so use the opportunity to make him an offer he can't refuse. He'll
probably insist that you discuss buying his Water Works,
but when he sees that you are more interested in something else, he may come around to what you really want
to buy.

The next salesman's talent that we are concerned with
is his knowledge of his wares. A salesman knows what

he is selling and knows how valuable his product is to his customers. If the salesman is selling something which the buyer cannot find anywhere else, he keeps this in mind when he determines what price to ask. If he is trying to sell something which the customer really doesn't need and can get from almost anyone, his chances of making a profitable sale are small. A salesman also knows approximately how much his customer is willing and able to pay for what he is selling. If he's really an expert, he also knows his product's true value to his buyer. A salesman in a Monopoly game should have most, if not all, of the knowledge about his product that a salesman in the real world has.

Mr. Expert always knows what he has to sell and what he needs to buy. His big advantage over his opponents is that he is not limited to trading and selling only property. He can sell all sorts of things and is knowledgeable about the weaknesses and strong points of what he is selling. In short, one of the biggest things a good trader in Monopoly has going for him is *knowledge*. He has more of it, and it is more highly refined than that of his opponents. Although his opponents might realize that Mr. Expert seems to know what he is doing, they also respect him and trust him for it. Since most players don't believe there is much skill to the game anyway, Mr. Expert is usually in a very good position to use his knowledge to his best advantage.

However, Mr. Expert has more than just knowledge of more imaginative items to offer in trade. He also has the shrewdness and calculating power of a used-car salesman when he analyzes the true value of the deals he offers and receives. Having been well trained to analyze investments and recognize the snares of the sugar-coated trade, he is a hard person to take advantage of. Most important of all, Mr. Expert knows that he has the ability to change the value of any trade by manipulating the circumstances surrounding the trade. For example, Mr. Expert:

1. Will try to soak up the houses immediately after he trades a new color group to his opponent.

2. Will try to obtain free lands that he is sure will not become worthless later on.

3. Will try to exaggerate the glamour of those color groups which he knows his opponents are not in a position to exploit.

The final important trait of a salesman is his delivery, or his ability to "talk" the trade. There are many words that can be used to express the same proposal. The words "option" and "partnership" can simply terrify some players. In such cases, the smart trader will avoid such terms and explain the same concept in a different vocabulary. A good trader adapts to his opponent's frame of mind. His language is phrased to say what he wants to say, in such a way that his opponent hears what *he* wants to hear. That's no easy trick!

Every player has a trading style all his own. This varies from the player who is content to sit back and roll the dice, not saying a word, to our friend Larry Loudmouth, who can never shut up. A good trader must observe and learn the trading style of his opponents if he hopes to adapt successfully. This is mostly a matter of getting a feel for the different types of traders in the game. Here are a few of the most common types which you are liable to run into, and some advice on how to handle them.

1. The player who, like Cathy Cautious, never trades at all, but would much rather collect $16 rent on St. James Place and $2 rent on Mediterranean Avenue. He refuses to consider any of the possible advantages to be gained from trading and is convinced that winning is a result only of pure luck. His biggest thrill is giving $4 change from a $20 bill. If you run into one of these guys, do your best, but don't be surprised if you can't budge him. If he's really immovable then use that knowledge when you trade with the other players. It's not really much of a danger to give another player a good trading position with this Rock of Gibraltar, since the likelihood

that he will be able to exploit this trading position and hurt you is very small.

2. The player who goes after one color group (or if he's especially odd, the Railroads) and is then content to never trade. This type of player is usually quite insane in his desire to acquire his favorite color group, and he has every intention of making horrendous trades to get what he wants. If you have what he wants, then don't sell cheap. If you don't have what he wants, don't waste time trying to reason with him; your efforts are better directed toward trying to get a property which he wants badly.

3. The player who doesn't trust his own mother. He has been tricked before and vowed never to let it happen again. (He probably grew up in a big city.) This type of player thinks that you're always out to trick him, and would much rather be safe than fooled. His pride would never let him risk humiliation if there is a way to lose peacefully. Although his attitude can usually be overcome, he can still be a major obstacle to your quick-moving, smooth trading game. The best thing to do is to try to gain this person's confidence. Offer a deal that is not too important to your strategy. When he refuses, reverse the terms of the deal and offer it in the opposite direction (for example, "I'll sell you my Railroad for $500. No? Then how about if I buy *your* Railroad for $500?"). By showing that you are willing to take either side of your offer, you can display your good faith and fairness. Even if he thinks that both possibilities are bad trades, you will still have made it clear that you are not out to cheat him.

4. The player who is really a frustrated banker. All he wants is money, money, and more money. He'd sell his soul for a crisp new $500 bill. He doesn't care about property unless it has big rents, and will practically give away a small color group. He is always a sucker for the glamourous high-rent properties, whether or not he can develop them. To best deal with this type, go along with his faulty logic. Tell him that he likes expensive properties and you like the cheap ones. Say that you're always

willing to trade away one expensive property for several cheap ones! It won't be hard to convince this guy to sell you Oriental Avenue, a measley Light Blue property, for $200 when he paid only $100 for it. Don't look a gift horse in the mouth!

5. The player who is compulsively clean—Mr. Nice-and-Neat. He doesn't really want to play Monopoly. All he wants to do is keep his money stacked up in nice, neat piles. If you sneeze, don't do it in his direction or you'll be his enemy for life. As far as his properties are concerned, the only reason he wants a complete color group is because things look nicer that way. Don't be surprised if he sells you a property dirt cheap because it clashes with the rest of his colors. When he sells cheap, just make sure that it's you, and not your opponents, who are doing the buying. He can be a very good friend, so it's best to humor him and help him to achieve his goals. If it's his Monopoly set, *never* write your option or free land agreement on the back of a $1 bill; get some scrap paper and keep it handy during the game instead. Finally, always pay this chap with your least crinkled money. He might pay you back with a property later.

6. The player who offers the most unreasonable one-sided deals imaginable—Larry Loudmouth. He is a firm believer in the "something-for-nothing" theory. He tells you he's being generous when he offers to relieve you of the responsibility of owning a property. You saw earlier how to take advantage of his offers if he has something you really need. How do you handle this type of player if he really doesn't have anything which you can use? Use him for image-building with the other players! Your best strategy against him is to offer counterproposals even more ridiculous than the offer he gave you. In this way, you throw his insulting proposals right back into his face. To get the full diplomatic effect, your counteroffer should be made with a serious tone and a sincere expression. It is immensely satisfying to see this type of player sputter helplessly about the unfairness and stupidity of your proposals.

The list of different types of weirdos could go on and on. In a sense, every player has his own odd preferences, and after all, a lot of the fun of the game is the crazy zeal with which some people play. However, do not let your own emotional antics or irrational dislikes get in the way of your strategies for winning. If you want to win consistently, you're going to have to sacrifice your own little "pet" habits.

It's now time to go over some of the essential fine points of negotiating tactics. The following tips can make the difference between being a somewhat successful salesman and being a professional salesman. There is no substitute for a true professional. To really master the art of diplomacy, the fine points must be understood just as clearly as the major ones.

ALWAYS KEEP YOUR OBJECTIVES IN MIND. This is the same advice that was given regarding general strategy. Since trading is one way of implementing your strategy, it is important to remember the direction in which you're going when you are surrounded by the diverting temptations of your opponents' offers. Listen carefully. Your opponent will probably expect to be forced to compromise anyway. If there is any part of his proposal which fits into your plans very well, make a counterproposal which preserves that part of his offer without as many sacrifices on your part. The closer your counteroffer is to your opponent's original proposal, the greater the likelihood that he will accept your counterproposal. So listen before you interrupt. Who knows? Your opponent may be offering just what you want!

PROPOSE TRADES WHICH APPEAR TO BE MUTUALLY BENEFICIAL. Your opponent knows that your goal in the game is not to help *him* win, but to help yourself win. He won't trust a deal which looks like you're giving up everything and receiving nothing in return. You should not offer deals which look "too good" on the surface. Likewise, you should be immediately suspicious of such offers from other players. A truly good deal looks good for both traders, and each realizes that the other is getting something which he wants. Don't trust an opponent if he offers a deal in which it looks like he's not gaining anything. The Trojan Horse has its counterparts in a Monopoly game.

BE HONEST WHEN YOU TRADE—OR AT LEAST APPEAR HONEST. Nothing is more convincing than the truth. Explain that any trade you offer has its advantages and disadvantages for each player involved. Then stress the advantages and deemphasize the disadvantages! Your opponents will expect a certain amount of exaggeration, just don't overdo it. Remember, you want to be the owner of the color group if you decide to form a partnership, but you don't really want to explain that the reason you're willing to pay for the building costs is to acquire the bankrupting power. You can be honest, while simultaneously steering discussion away from the advantages which you stand to gain from the trade.

ESTABLISH YOUR CREDIBILITY. Other players will always do business with you if you have a good record. Your reputation for making "fair deals" does not have to be destroyed just because you manage to win every game. After all, most players will attribute your victories to good luck, and you'll be the first to agree with them. Having a good reputation for honest dealings can make winning a lot easier. But don't think that your reputation will suffer if you insist on strict adherence to the terms of any trade you make. If you promised a player half the rent you collect and you decide not to collect it, he is not entitled to any money from you. If there is any fuss, ask the other players to come to your aid. A deal is a deal!

ALWAYS START WITH THE WORST OFFER YOU CAN MAKE WHICH SOUNDS REASONA-

BLE—YOU CAN ALWAYS COMPROMISE LAT-ER. Whenever you are bargaining over a price, bid your lowest offer and ask your highest selling price. If you don't leave room for compromise, many players will not buy or sell—no matter how fair the price that you are offering or asking is. Play it safe and start at the extremes. Who knows? Maybe you'll get a bargain!

INTRODUCE NEW CONCEPTS GENTLY. If your opponents are unfamiliar with options, free lands, revenue sharing, immunity, etc., be patient and reassuring when you introduce them into the game. Many people play Monopoly with their own "house rules," some of which are so common that the players think that their own variations are actually part of the official Parker Brothers rules. When you explain some of the advanced concepts, be sure to stress that they are perfectly legal and that they are commonly used where you come from, or in many other parts of the country.

Do not be arrogant or try to seem superior when you explain how something like an option agreement works. Act mildly surprised that your opponents have never heard of one, and explain the process as if it were just another good idea. Be careful. Some players are especially resistant to anything new. If necessary, you have enough skill with the fundamentals of the game to be a consistant winner, even without a lot of the advanced strategies. The game's much livelier if you can use imaginative concepts, however, so emphasize that (a) private agreements cannot be outlawed between two players who want to make them, and (b) private agreements with imagination make the game much more fun, much more challenging, and much less time-consuming.

DON'T HARASS YOUR OPPONENTS. Don't bother an opponent over and over again with the same idea that he has refused each of the previous three times you suggested it. Bide your time, and don't let your opponent know how much you're dying to get that property of his. All you'll accomplish by repeating your offer is to make him more aware of the true value of that property, a move which could make him raise the price even more. One deal, proposed and explained at the right time, is much more effective than continuous nagging. If it's a real emergency, some sarcastic muttering to yourself about players who came to roll the dice, not to trade, might be helpful. In general, however, if you have to ask more than twice, you'd better start thinking of alternate ways to get what you want.

DON'T BE AFRAID TO VERBALLY INTIMIDATE A PEST. If another player tries to interfere with your negotiations, don't let him. Every player should have a right to express his opinion, since any trade affects every player in the game either directly or indirectly. However, some rules of courtesy should be respected in order to prevent riots and keep the game enjoyable. If you are trying to make a deal and another player interrupts, tell him that you will be happy to let him comment on your trade as soon as you are finished explaining it. This will keep things under control and bolster your image as a fair, open-minded player. In addition, once you have convinced your opponent of the mutual benefits of your proposal, any additions or interference on the part of the other players will have to be very accurate in order to have any effect.

On the other side of the board, if your opponents are making trades, do not be afraid to ridicule the terms of the deal and to try to prevent them from reaching an agreement, remaining courteous at all times, of course. If you can see that you will not be able to stop your opponents from reaching a fair agreement, then it is good diplomacy to agree that the deal is "pretty good for both of you." In this way, you can again reinforce your image as an honest and fair trader. Don't waste your energy trying to stop the inevitable. Just capitalize on it!

DON'T BE OVERANXIOUS TO COMPLETE A TRADE. Nothing makes an opponent more nervous than an eager beaver saying, "Okay, okay. It's a deal.

Here, take the money, now gimme the property." This can only make your opponent certain that he's being cheated in some way. When it appears that you have been able to reach an agreement with your opponent, casually review the terms of the trade and offer your half, saying something to the effect of, "Well, I guess that sounds fair to me." If your opponent seems reluctant, offer some reassuring words. Sometimes it pays to appear reluctant yourself. There's no harm in letting your opponent think he's pressured you into a deal, even if that's not exactly what happened.

Remember that no deal is complete until both players have positively agreed to it and whatever concessions were part of the agreement have changed hands. It is not uncommon for players to back out at the last minute. If it looks like this is happening to you, don't panic. If he was willing to accept your offer at first, it shouldn't take too much coaxing on your part to get him to accept again. You might have to sweeten your offer by another $100, but not much more. Sometimes a little verbal pressure can go a long way.

Happy trading!

CHAPTER 10 SUMMARY

   I. When to speak up:
      A. Bargaining from weakness.
      B. The aggressive player
  II. Knowing how to pursue a bargain.
 III. Knowing what you're selling.
  IV. Knowing how to sell it.
   V. Different types of players.
  VI. Keep your objectives in mind.
 VII. Emphasize mutual benefits.
VIII. Be honest—or appear honest.
  IX. Introduce new concepts slowly.
   X. Don't harass.
  XI. Don't be overanxious.

The Balance of Power—Your Opponents Are Your Best Friends

Did you ever play or watch a children's game called King of the Hill? All you need are a hill and several kids who are willing to engage in a little rowdy fun. The rules are simple: try to be the only person at the top of the hill by throwing everyone else off. Once you get to be the top guy, it's pretty difficult to stay there. If you're strong enough, you can beat your challengers off one at a time and maintain your position as "king of the hill." However, if two or three challengers get together and rush from different directions at the same time . . . well, there's usually a new "king of the hill." The fundamental principles that apply to this rough game also apply to an even rougher game: Monopoly.

The trick to being a winner at King of the Hill is making sure that (*a*) you are as strong as, or stronger than, each individual opponent, and (*b*) your opponents never get together to push you off the hill. Things are no different in Monopoly. Each game is a *balance of power,* where one or more players develop stronger positions than the others, and the other players try to conspire to dethrone them. How many times have you heard (or said yourself), "I'm not trading with you. You've already got all of those properties; and look at all your money!" When a player trades selectively, he is demonstrating his knowledge of the importance of a balance of power in the game.

At any given instant, there are only four ways in which a Monopoly game can be developing:

1. Nobody is winning. There is no clear leader, because it's too early in the game or because nobody has really managed to take a significant lead over all the other players.

2. *You are winning, but nobody's doing anything about it.* Either your opponents haven't noticed that you're winning yet, or even better, they have given up any hope of beating you and are fighting among themselves for second place.

3. *You are winning, and everybody's trying to do something about it.* One or two players refuse to have anything to do with you with regard to trading. Your opponents are getting ready to see if they can't all cooperate to destroy your dominant position.

4. *One of your opponents is winning.*

WHAT TO DO IF NOBODY IS WINNING. (There is no "king of the hill.")

At the beginning of the game, there is an even balance of power, until a stronger player emerges. Follow your Monopoly instincts. Often, however, a game develops into a situation where although there is no clear leader, two players are clearly better off than are the other two. In such a game, if you are one of those players who are ahead, your strategy is to undermine the position of your co-leader, preferably by cooperating with the other players. If you are not one of the two leaders, try to sow the seeds of disunity between them. Don't panic. Your superior skill should soon displace them.

WHAT TO DO IF YOU ARE WINNING AND NOBODY ELSE KNOWS, OR NOBODY ELSE CARES. (You're "king of the hill," but the other players haven't gotten together yet.)

This is the ideal position for a Monopoly player. When you are winning, the best thing that can happen is to have your opponents believe that someone else is winning. It can be very complicated to determine who is leading at any given moment. However, a good player can look at an average game and form a general estimation of who is on top. By now, you have more than enough knowledge to do over-the-board analysis. Hopefully, when you look at your game, you will see that you are winning.

But the fact that you are winning does not mean that everyone else realizes it. If your opponents think that someone else is winning, great! *A smart player never makes a target of himself unless it is absolutely necessary.*

Sometimes it takes some ingenuity to convince other players that you're not winning when the truth of the matter is that you are. If you haven't guessed by now, Monopoly games can be very cutthroat. Although you should never lie about the facts of your financial position (properties, cash, etc.), a little well-placed misdirection concerning your knowledge of who is "winning" can be essential. Some of the following statements might come in handy for convincing your opponents that you're not the one they should really be out to get:

a. "How about Val over there? She's the one who's winning! Look at her! She's got hotels on her Light Blue group, and she's got all that cash! All I have is three houses on my Reds *(be careful not to say "three houses on each Red" or "nine houses"),* and haven't got half the cash that she's got. I still say we should team up to get her while we can."

b. "What about Albert sitting back with that devious little smile of his? Look at all those title deed cards he's got! See how he keeps them in a pile so he doesn't advertise to the rest of us that he has so many! He's winning, not me!"

c. "Me? Winning? You've lost your mind! Look at sweet little Maxine sitting quietly behind all those $500 bills. Now I may be no judge, and neither is she, but how could anyone say that I'm winning when she's got thousands and thousands of dollars. If I had that much money, then I'd be more than happy to face my critics and say I'm winning. She may say she's in a delicate position, but let's give credit where credit is due!"

d. "You think I'm winning? Are we playing the same game, or do you just need new glasses? Look at Champion Lee's position. Okay, I may own some Oranges with some houses, but that's just an ice cream store compared with his Sears Roebuck over there. Don't get fooled just because they don't have any houses on them yet. As soon as he gets some cash, we're all going to be sunk. If there's anything we should do, it's make sure that he doesn't get his hands on any cash."

These are a few examples of creative finger-pointing. Exclamations like these can often buy large amounts of valuable time by misleading your opponents. Keep a low profile so as not to attract attention. If you have a lot of money, there's no reason for you to flash it around. Always keep your smaller bills on top of your money pile, as indicated before. Remember the words of the famous Cornell scholar Elliott Millenson: *"The right image is like money in the bank."*

Sometimes your efforts to hide your power fail. Often there is no way you can possibly expect any of your opponents to believe that you are not far ahead of everyone else. In this situation, it becomes necessary to use some delicate balance-of-power strategy.

WHAT TO DO IF YOU ARE WINNING AND EVERYONE ELSE IS TRYING TO DO SOMETHING ABOUT IT. (For some reason nobody is singing "God Save the King.")

It has been said that it's hard to teach a person how to make money, but it's twice as hard to teach him how to keep it. This is nowhere truer than in a Monopoly game. When you suddenly find that your skillful trading and shrewd investments have paid off in a winning position, you are apt to feel mighty proud of yourself. You have managed to play better than any of your opponents!

But now the real test comes. Can you play better than all of your opponents put together? The only way to answer a confident "yes" to this question is to use one of two possible strategies, depending on the situation:

1. Forget about your strongest opponent and concentrate on being the first player to bankrupt the weaker opponents.

2. Use every resource at your command to keep your weakest opponents alive while you concentrate your efforts on bankrupting or severely weakening the strongest opponent (the balance-of-power principle).

The first strategy is nice, simple, and straightforward. The idea is to go out and bankrupt your opponents. It has a flaw in a complicated game, however. It becomes very dangerous to damage the position of one of the weaker players and set him up for bankruptcy. If one of your other opponents is significantly stronger than the rest, there is a chance that he might get lucky and bankrupt the player whom *you* set up. In this case, he would acquire all of that player's properties and become a major threat to your position. The skilled tournament player does not like to take such big risks. For this reason, he uses this first strategy only if he has significantly more bankrupting power than his strongest opponent. Otherwise, he resorts to the second strategy, balance of power.

At first, this second strategy seems self-defeating. It says that you must not try to eliminate your opponents, but try to keep some of them in the game! Why? Because in any game where you are winning and there is only one serious threat to your position, it can be a good idea to keep your opponents in the game *as long as they are hurting that threat more than they are hurting you.* Here is the simplest type of balance-of-power strategy in action.

Dick	*Stan*	*Mr. Expert*
The Red group	The Yellow group	The Green group
3 Houses on each	4 Houses on each	Hotels on each
Boardwalk	Park Place	The Maroon group
$500 cash	$1500 cash	3 Houses on each
		$3000 cash

This is the crux of a three-player finish of a fairly normal Monopoly game. Mr. Expert is clearly ahead. Both Dick and Stan realize that Mr. Expert will win unless they act together. However, there are several reasons why they haven't gotten together yet on Boardwalk and Park Place. They are both greedy and want to own the color group; Stan thinks that he can bankrupt Dick if he waits (Mr. Expert told him so); and both Dick and Stan realize that they will have great difficulties finding the houses to build on the Dark Blues (Mr. Expert discreetly pointed this out too). They have decided to wait for a little while longer.

Suppose Dick (owner of the Reds) lands on Mr. Expert's Green group and owes him $1275. Mr. Expert's first reaction is to make Dick pay up. But he looks again and sees that he doesn't really need the money, so he offers to accept Boardwalk instead of the rent (this would prevent Dick and Stan from ever teaming up on the Dark Blues). Dick thinks for a moment, listens to Stan scream about not playing into Mr. Expert's hands, and then tells Mr. Expert that he will not give up Boardwalk. Mr. Expert replies that if Dick doesn't, he will be forced to sell his only source of income—the houses on the Red group. "And once you've sold those houses, you have no chance of ever raising the money to put them back up," says Mr. Expert.

But Dick just smiles, for he thinks he knows a reason why Mr. Expert will never collect the rent money form him! Has Dick made a terrible error, or does he really know a reason why Mr. Expert shouldn't collect that $1275?

Dick's a pretty smart player. He realizes that there are two reasons why it would be stupid for Mr. Expert to collect that rent and force him to tear down those houses.

1. If Dick pays $1275, he will be severely weakened. In fact, his position will be weakened so badly that if he lands on Stan's Yellow group, he will go bankrupt. The one thing that Mr. Expert wants to avoid is having Stan bankrupt Dick. If Stan were allowed to get new properties to use against Mr. Expert, then he would have a much better chance to win. Therefore, it is in Mr. Expert's best interests not to weaken Dick to the point where there is a serious danger of his going bankrupt to Stan. He should collect only enough rents to keep Dick

from getting too strong, until he has ruined Stan's chances of bankrupting Dick.

2. Mr. Expert is trying to beat his major threat, Stan, at the moment. Mr. Expert realizes that Dick's Red group is helping Mr. Expert to weaken Stan's position. Whenever Stan lands on Dick's Reds, he pays Dick enough to be constantly short of cash. If Mr. Expert were to force Dick to sell the houses on the Reds, he would be helping Stan! The question he asks himself is, "Do the houses on that color group hurt me more than they hurt my more dangerous opponent?" In this example, the Red group is hurting Stan much more than it is hurting Mr. Expert. Therefore, he should not force Dick to sell those houses.

Notice that in this situation it would be very foolish for Dick to make any trade with Stan in which Dick would give Stan immunity on the Red group. In this case, Dick would have outlived his usefulness to Mr. Expert, since he would no longer be hurting Stan. If he were to do this, he'd better be strong enough to stand on his own two feet. If Dick starts to rock the boat, Mr. Expert can, and should, let Dick go bankrupt. At the moment, however, Dick knows very well that Mr. Expert can't really afford to make him sell his houses.

Suppose, however, that Mr. Expert isn't as smart as Dick and does not see why he shouldn't charge Dick the full rent. If this were to happen, then *Dick should explain to Mr. Expert why he shouldn't charge the rent.* Mr. Expert will understand Dick's reasoning and realize that it is not worth the risk of seeing Stan bankrupt Dick to get a handful of cash (which, in fact, is best invested in houses on Dick's Reds, even for Mr. Expert).

In your games, however, be careful. A balance of power is a complex strategic concept, and many players will never understand the logic behind not collecting a large rent, no matter how clearly you explain it. Expect to have large difficulties implementing this strategy if it becomes necessary to explain it to other players. Usually, however, such explanations will be unnecessary.

There is one major exception to the balance-of-power

strategy in this situation. If Mr. Expert found that he could actually bankrupt Dick by making him pay the full rent, and assuming there was no way that Dick could trade to raise the needed cash, then Mr. Expert should by all means bankrupt him. After all, this would give Mr. Expert an entire Red group with plenty of cash to develop it. Balance-of-power strategies rarely apply to bankrupting situations.

As you can see, a player who wants to be an expert has to break away from more traditional ways of thinking about winning. Sometimes it is to your advantage not to collect rent. The farther ahead you get, the more likely your opponents will be to band together to tear you down. Before you upset a balance in which you are winning, be sure to weigh the consequences of your activities. Consider all the possible factors before deciding what is really in your best interests. Sometimes you would much rather have houses sitting on one opponent's Light Blues than on another opponent's Greens. In this case, hold off on bankrupting him or otherwise forcing him to flood the market with those houses until you are sure that the player with the Greens will never be able to get them. Always minimize the risk that anyone will go bankrupt to any other player but you. There is really no substitute for practice if you want to acquire skill in manipulating the balance of power and "putting the game away" when you're winning.

WHAT TO DO IF YOU ARE LOSING. ("Down with the King!")

Before you apply balance-of-power principles to improving your losing position, it is important to first analyze why you are behind at all. Then, just as a doctor who has diagnosed a disease is more able to prescribe a cure, so will it be much easier for you to go to work on remedying your situation.

There is really only one way to be in serious trouble in a Monopoly game: one or more of your opponents have a color group, but you do not. This is the most common reason for bankruptcy in games between average players. This should rarely happen to good players, however, especially if they are playing against less skillful opponents. If one of your opponents has obtained, and perhaps even begun to develop, a color group, then you should get moving right away. Using a little balance-of-power psychology, point out that it is important that the rest of the players get together on trades before it is too late. Try to create a feeling of solidarity among the players who don't own color groups. Isolate the leading opponent, portraying him as a "common enemy." If you succeed in convincing the rest of the players that they should forget their own petty jealousies to destroy the common enemy, you will find trading a lot easier. If you have been playing shrewdly, by buying options and trading to acquire property, it won't be long before you have your own color group. Do not stop referring to that early leader as the common enemy until the last possible moment. A Monopoly game involves psychological warfare as well as economic warfare—a good player is prepared to fight both battles.

Even if you can avoid such serious troubles, it is still possible for you to be in second place during a game. This usually will happen when your major opponent has a color group with more profit-earning power than yours has. Assuming that both color groups are fully developed, your opponent has the advantage for the moment. There are three steps that you can take to improve your position to a winning one. The first two are offensive tactics, the third is a defensive one:

1. Try to form a partnership with one of the weaker players. Naturally, you should be the owner. If you are not winning when you suggest forming the partnership, you will probably have to make the terms quite lucrative for your partner. In order to get a weak player to surrender a crucial completing property, you might offer one or two free lands on your already-developed color group, in addition to the usual immunity and half of the cash revenues on the new color group. If he doesn't go for these terms, replace the free land offer with one of a quarter, or even half, of the cash revenues on your first color group. The important thing is to get another color group to use against your major opponent. Don't worry too much about what you promise the weak player, since either (a) he'll go bankrupt soon enough anyway, or (b) once you get powerful enough, you can trade away the color groups and destroy his interest in them. Just be certain that, if he has any other properties which are valuable to either you or your major opponent, you will have a way of ensuring that you will still be able to bankrupt him.

2. *Whenever one of the weaker players lands on your developed color group and you can't bankrupt him, then accept property in lieu of the debt. or try to make a trade which would include cancellation of the rent.* In theory, you should have been doing this all along, but if you are losing, redouble your efforts. Remember, your opponents will be more eager to trade when they suddenly owe you a nice chunk of cash. Always go for color properties—never utilities, and rarely Railroads.

3. *Make sure that weak players with important properties do not go bankrupt to anyone but you!* When necessary, help your opponents to pay debts to other players just to keep them from going bankrupt. Buy worthless options on things like the Water Works to get them the money they need. Be careful not to say that the reason that you are helping them is to let them go bankrupt to you. Such forms of two-faced altruism might upset many players. Remember that you need your opponents' properties to win, so their interests are often your interests.

One final word on balance of power. Always do your best to stop your opponents from trading or otherwise teaming up. Ridicule them, play on their greed, and make your own counteroffers. But be careful not to interrupt them or be so obnoxious that you ruin your credibility. Sometimes there will be no choice, and you will have to sit and take your lumps. However, the more you can prevent your opponents from teaming up, the less danger there is of their overpowering you. Use the balance of power in order to ensure that the scales of victory are tipped in your favor.

CHAPTER 11 SUMMARY

   I. The four types of games:
      A. Nobody's winning.
      B. You're winning and nobody knows.
      C. You're winning and everybody knows.
      D. Somebody else is winning.
  II. Never make a target of yourself.
 III. The balance-of-power principle.
 IV. Self-interest.
  V. Teaming up to win.

The Beauty of Bankruptcy

Bankruptcy is the American nightmare. Some people will steal from the blind, swindle their loved ones, or sell their souls before admitting financial defeat. It's a strange combination of societal attitudes and human motivation that casts shame on those who go bankrupt. We are taught to admire success and to let the free marketplace punish the unsuccessful with financial ruin. Thank goodness Monopoly is only a game, not a life-and-death situation. Naturally, you try your hardest to win, but most mature people can always keep things in perspective. Every now and then, however . . .

For some reason, people can get very emotional and highly irrational when playing Monopoly. Perhaps one of the reasons for such strange behavior is that the object is to ruin and bankrupt your opponents. If you want to win, you must often mercilessly draw every last dollar from your best friend, girlfriend, or employer. Very few people lose with a smile, and Monopoly games have been known to break up marriages and romances. It's "Everyone for himself and woe to he who crosses my path!" There have been times when players, needing only a few dollars' rent, have offered to make up the difference in real U.S. currency! The creditor, of course, wanted the thrill of victory more than he wanted a few dollars, and he took great pleasure in declining. Madness!

In spite of all this, the fact of the matter is that most players do not understand the whole process of bankruptcy in a Monopoly game, and you can use this fact to your advantage. While some people play their whole game trying only to avoid bankruptcy, a smart player learns how to use other players' fears, irrationalities, and ignorance to help himself to end up the winner.

What are the important ways in which bankruptcy affects the game? The primary effect of bankruptcy is the tremendous property shift which it brings about. A good player rarely, if ever, bankrupts only to get money. To think otherwise is a grave mistake. Property is the key to winning the game, and bankruptcy is the cheapest way to acquire property. Players usually go bankrupt because they owe only a few hundred dollars beyond what they can afford. For this reason, bankruptcy is often a time when property can be bought and sold at noncompetitive prices. The two major features of bankruptcy can be summarized as follows:

BANKRUPTCY IS THE MAJOR WAY TO ACQUIRE LARGE QUANTITIES OF PROPERTY.

BANKRUPTCY TEMPORARILY WARPS THE SUPPLY-AND-DEMAND PRICE LAWS (IT CREATES BARGAINS).

These two points will be the basis of the discussion later in the chapter. First, let's review the rules behind bankruptcy. They leave a loophole with regard to the question of *when* a player is actually bankrupt.

The official rules say: *"A player is bankrupt when he owes more than he can pay. If his debt is to another player, he must turn over to that player all that he has of value and retire from the game."*

The vagueness of the phrase "when he owes more than he can pay" has led to many arguments over when a player is declared bankrupt. There are two fairly opposite lines of reasoning on this point.

The basic interpretation, endorsed by Parker Brothers, is that if a player can raise the necessary money before his turn is over, by last-minute trading, then he does not owe more than he "can pay" and is not bankrupt. In other words, if you owe a large rent, you are allowed to do whatever you can to scrape up the rent money by using your ingenuity and sales skills. However, if you cannot raise the money, you must give your creditor all that you had of value *when you rolled the dice and landed on the property,* since at that moment you owed more than you could pay. You cannot, in a move of revenge, sell all of your properties to some other player for $1 and then give that dollar to your creditor in an admission of bankruptcy. A player has an opportunity to prove that he does not owe more than he is *capable of paying,* but if he is unable to prove this by raising the money, then he is bankrupt as of the moment that he incurs the debt.

The second interpretation is a literal interpretation and can serve as a major loophole. It says that if a player cannot, by selling his houses to the Bank and mortgaging his property, raise enough money to pay his rent, then he "owes more than he can pay" and is bankrupt as of that moment. It gives a debtor no opportunity to make trades to pull himself out of debt at the last minute. This is a highly restrictive definition, one which seems unnecessarily harsh. At times, it may be necessary to use this interpretation to collect rent from a player who in a fit of poor sportsmanship is trying to illegally give all his properties away. However, in general, it is very risky to use this interpretation, since sooner or later you will find yourself knocking on bankruptcy's door. Then it will be rather difficult to return to a more liberal definition. In general, stick with the freer interpretation, which keeps your options open, since you are probably in a better position to exploit those options than your opponents are.

For the purposes of strategy in this chapter, we will use only the first interpretation of the rules.

What do you do if someone lands on your developed property and owes more than he can pay without trading?

1. You must make an immediate decision: is there any reason not to quickly and peacefully bankrupt this player? The only time you would not want to bankrupt him would be if there were overriding balance-of-power considerations. Let's assume that you want to bankrupt him.

2. Do not, *do not,* jump up and down with glee, yelling, "I told you so," or other insults, unless such actions are absolutely necessary to maintain your honor and satisfy your basic animal urges. Instead, it is much safer to smile, be courteous and sympathetic, and try to get his properties before he gets any ideas about trying to sell some of them to raise the money he needs. Try to act as if it's too bad that he's bankrupt, but you really can't see anything that he can do. Let him know that you're pretty sure that his cause is futile. If he has houses, calmly start to add up how much money he gains by selling them to the Bank at half price. If your debtor snarls at you as you count his houses, back down and explain that you were only trying to be helpful. (*Note: some players have such intense pride that they develop an emotional attachment to the houses they build on their properties, and any attempt by you to destroy those houses can precipitate a violent reaction.*)

3. If your attempts at a quiet, rapid settlement of the situation fail, you will find yourself with a very delicate problem. All those vultures we mentioned before will come to life when they see another player about to go bankrupt. The bankrupt player might have that last Maroon property or that fourth Railroad, and this is bad news for you. The entire game can come to life, with dozens of proposals being hurled at the bankrupted player. If it looks as if your debtor is going to be able to raise the money he owes you by selling some of his valuable properties, you must forget all about bankruptcy and concentrate on getting one or two good properties for yourself in exchange for a promise to waive the rent. (The only exception to this rule is when you need the cash so badly that without it you stand a good chance of being driven bankrupt yourself.) The fact that your

debtor owes you so much money puts you in an excellent position to say something like, "I'm willing to keep you alive in this game if you give me the Orange and the Light Blue properties." If your offer is reasonable, the debtor will usually be happy to deal directly with you.

4. Sometimes, however, things don't go exactly as planned. Because a Monopoly game always brings out strong emotions, your opponent could try to use all sorts of unsportsmanlike maneuvers to deprive you of your victory. If it looks like he is about to use one of the following dirty tricks, you must spring into action immediately!

a. He might, as we mentioned before, try to sell all of his property to another player for $1, and then give that dollar to you. If he tries this old ploy to deprive the victor of his spoils, explain that the rules say that he is bankrupt "when he owes more than he can pay." Either he can pay it or he can't. If he can't pay the debt, then he is bankrupt as of the time he lands on the property, and all that he owns of value at that time must be turned over to his creditor. If logic fails, we suggest that in the future you find more mature companions with whom to play.

b. He might decide to leave in style and throw the board, the Bank, and all the properties into the air. Stand back—those flying houses can hurt. Just remember that it's not worth beating someone who can not behave in a civilized manner if he loses.

c. He might threaten your life. This is not as uncommon as you might think. In such a situation, it is important that you first decide whether or not he is serious. If there is *any chance that he is serious,* then by all means waive the rent. The crucial strategy in this situation is to live so that you will be able to win future Monopoly games. Once your opponent has calmed down a bit, excuse yourself to go to the bathroom and leave the building as quickly as possible. Out a window, if necessary. Don't come back for a week.

If you are certain that your opponent is only exaggerating, then do not let yourself be intimidated. Be firm.

Neither threats nor hisses should change your mind. Remember that if you don't bankrupt a weak player, the next player may not be so sympathetic. He might snatch all those valuable properties and use them against you. The same advice applies if your opponent begins to cry and plead. Be firm and end his misery quickly. Nice guys don't always finish last, but they seldom finish first.

That's the best situation—where someone is going bankrupt to you. What about the less favorable possibilities?

The second possible bankrupting situation is where one of your opponents is going bankrupt to another opponent. Whenever this happens, the first word which should pop into your mind is "Bargains!" There is a very simple reason for the way this situation brings about an opportunity to gain property cheaply—a player who is about to go bankrupt needs the money fast and is in no position to argue about trivial things like an extra free land on Mediterranean Avenue. However, there are two things which must be considered when you negotiate with a person who is in a state of "imminent bankruptcy."

1. *Pride.* Many players would rather lose the game than sell their "valuable" properties at the "insulting" prices which you offer to pay. Be careful not to take total advantage of your opponent's predicament when you propose your offers. If a player is desperate and offers you a property at a bargain price, don't hassle him to reduce his prices just because he's in trouble. Nobody likes a parasite who profits from other people's misfortunes. If you behave like a greedy hog, a losing player might well decide that he has been playing long enough and go bankrupt without ever selling you any properties. Bankruptcy can make people irrational. Don't push them. You might end up pushing them to use the excuse, "I'm tired of playing this game. Since I'm bankrupt, I might as well quit now."

At this point, we might as well mention a related

problem which can put a real dent in your plans for victory. If the game has dragged on for a few hours, a player might decide he's getting tired and want to give all his properties to the underdog. If this about to happen, it's really unfair for you to insist that he sit down and play until he goes bankrupt. You *can* insist that he not give all his properties to a person who would be the least likely to bankrupt him if he stayed in the game. A compromise which you could suggest is that he turn over all his properties and money to the Bank. It's not perfect, but at least it gives all the remaining players an even shot at getting those properties.

2. *A stake in the game.* Related to considerations of pride, every player must feel that he has some chance of winning if he is going to make an effort to avoid going bankrupt. For this reason, make sure that any trade you propose during this critical period will leave the player who is in trouble with the appearance of some significant chance of winning. Don't guarantee him victory; just don't make it appear totally impossible for him to pull a win out of the fire. When trying to make trades with a person who is wavering between resignation and playing on, it is important to stress the positive possibilities of his position. If you're playing with a jackpot, it's always a good idea to mention how one quick land on free parking could turn things around for him. Emphasize his stake in the game, and you will increase your chances of picking up a good deal for yourself.

Some players are such fierce competitors that they believe that as long as they are still moving their tokens, they have a chance to win. These players are the best to deal with when they get in trouble. They will listen to any proposal you make them. If you see that one of these types is about to give up, a comment like, "Gee, I never thought you were a quitter," will usually bring him right back.

If you are aware of these two considerations, you are ready to try to bargain with the struggling opponent. Make it clear from the beginning that you are not trading with him only to watch him go bankrupt a few turns later. Show him that you actually want to help him stay in the game. Phrases like "You've been good to me when I was in trouble" and "That's not much rent—I can probably help you out" can work wonders. Maintain the upper hand when you are negotiating, while keeping the considerations of "pride" and "a stake in the game" in mind. Realize that if you trade fairly, you will enhance your reputation as a fair trader in good times and bad. That reputation could be the factor which causes your opponent to give up struggling when he lands on one of *your* properties—if he has to go broke, he might as well go broke to someone who is fair, as well as winning.

When dealing with a bankruptcy situation, don't forget about the player who is *collecting* the rent. Does he care only about getting his money, or is he much smarter than that? Often a skillful bankrupting player will not offer any sort of trade until it appears clear that the would-be bankrupted player will be able to trade property with somebody else and raise the necessary money. Why should he bid for property if he's going to get it for free if the player goes broke? But once it looks certain that you will be able to close a deal with the debtor, a smart creditor will step in with a better counteroffer, realizing that it's better to get property than a lot of useless money. If you are up against such an opponent, he will probably have a much stronger bargaining position than you, since he can offer to waive the debt (usually a large sum of money) in exchange for whatever it is that the debtor is selling. Don't try to fight him on his own terms. Convince the debtor that it is much better in the long run to deal with you, rather than to help build up the crushing, powerful position of his creditor. If, on the other hand, you find yourself facing an opponent who is more interested in collecting rent than collecting property, make sure that you profit from his mistake.

* * *

Having discussed all of the possible ways that your opponents can go bankrupt to either you or each other, it is time we considered the last alternative. What should you do when you are about to go bankrupt?

Hopefully, by applying what you have learned, you will avoid this problem. Eventually, however, the Fates will gang up against you, and you will need a solution to keep you fighting. In other situations, you may even deliberately allow yourself to drift into this precarious position in order to take advantage of its psychological value.

When you owe another player a large sum of money, there are three things that you can do:

1. Raise the cash yourself.

2. Convince one of your opponents to buy something worthless from you, giving you enough money to pay the debt.

3. Make an arrangement with your creditor so that he either waives the rent completely or accepts something in its place.

Let's assume for the time being that you can't raise the cash to pay the rent. Chapter 14 will be devoted entirely to the art of raising cash in an emergency, so there is no need to deal with it here. Besides, if you've got enough money to pay the debt, you're not under any real pressure anyway.

There are two alternatives left. It is not ridiculous to think about making your opponents raise some money on your behalf. Examine the position and ask yourself whether your bankruptcy will injure the positions of any other player in the game. If so, how? Monopoly players will not rush out to help someone just because he's going bankrupt, especially if they are paying large rents to that player on his well-developed color groups. However, no player wants to see another player win! The other players don't care at all if you go broke, but if your going broke will help someone else to win, then players will intervene to safeguard their own interests. They will be even more likely to do so if you *help them to realize what a danger your bankruptcy could be for them!* The chances are good that your creditor is the most powerful player in the game. Nobody wants to see the rich get richer, so speak up and start appealing to your opponents' own self-interests to get them to save you. Here are some sample pleas:

a. "Listen, Sue, if I don't get $400, I'm going to go broke to Ken, and I'll have to sell all of *our* houses on the Green group, from which you get half the profits! Furthermore, Ken has reams of money, and if he gets the Reds, he'll build on them himself. Then you'll be paying on the Greens *and* the Reds. You can't afford to see him get any more powerful!"

b. "My dear Lorraine, if I go bankrupt to Cindy, she gets all of my properties. That includes the third Orange property, which you want so badly. She's the leader already; you don't want her to get any stronger, do you? My position is pretty weak at the moment, since I owe $500, but you have plenty of money and a fully developed color group. I'm really not asking you to play St. Nicholas—it's in your own interest to help me out. If you help me pay this debt, you can keep me alive until I come around to your color group. Then you can bankrupt me! You want me to sell you the Orange property outright! I can't do that. I'd have no bargaining position left in the game if I did that. If I don't have at least some chance, there's no reason to play on. I might as well go bankrupt right now."

c. "Chuck, if I am forced to tear down these houses to pay my debt, we're both going to be in big trouble. True, I'll be in more trouble than you will, but look carefully at the position. If I tear down the houses on my Maroons, Michelle over here is going to snatch them up and put them on her Greens. Once I sell houses, there won't be a housing shortage anymore, and she'll use those houses to bankrupt you as well as me! By helping me pay this debt, you can keep the houses on the Maroons, where they are hurting her. We're going to have to cooperate a bit if we want to have any chance at all. Now look, I'm only $600 short, and . . ."

The trick to making other players pay all or part of

your debt is to explain clearly and *honestly* why it is in their best interests not to watch you go bankrupt. If you look hard enough, everybody has at least one reason for keeping you out of someone else's clutches. A Monopoly game brings out the greed in a lot of people. Since everyone is secretly wishing to bankrupt you himself, it is your job to exploit that desire. Nothing sells better in an argument than "self-interest" when it's sold carefully and correctly.

How exactly do you transfer the money from another player to yourself? If you can't convince him to buy a "Get out of Jail Free" card, a utility, or an option on a utility, then suggest trades which would include the money you need to pay your debt. In those trades, be sure that you don't give up anything you would not give up in a normal trade. The fact that you are in a weak position is no reason to make your position any weaker.

If all else fails, it's time to put a little pressure on the person who is causing you all of the trouble in the first place. Take a good look at your creditor's position. If all he's interested in is the cash, you're in trouble. In that case, you're going to have to convince him that you're worth more to him alive than dead, and that's no easy trick. You might try explaining that as long as you stay in the game, you keep on passing Go and collecting money which you pay him in the form of rents. Thus, the longer you're in the game, the more money he collects! Some people will believe any kind of reasoning that sounds logical!

Maybe he's not interested in your cash nearly as much as he's interested in bankrupting you to get that last Green property, the one that he really needs. There's only one way to find out. Pick it up and ask if anyone is interested in buying it. If your creditor's eyes suddenly light up, you know that you've found a possible way out of bankruptcy. Get another player to make some offer, any offer, for that property. Then you can start negotiating with your creditor over the terms of your upcoming trade. Try to make him forget that if no other players will deal with you, he will get that property by bankrupting you anyway. Let him know by the tone of your voice that you're doing him a great favor by negotiating with him. If he wants those Greens badly enough, and he loses sight of the fact that he'll get them if he doesn't say a word, you can do quite well for yourself. If there's no other way out, you can always give up the Green property if you're promised immunity on those Greens and a few free lands on the color group which caused you your present problems. The key to making a deal with an opponent who has you on the verge of bankruptcy is to find his weakness or secret desire and exploit it. Use the fact that you are going broke to your advantage. Argue, "Look, you can afford to give me Oriental Avenue as some compensation. Who am I? I'm so weak I'm almost broke. The least you can do while you trade with me is give me a break. You're so powerful that it couldn't possibly hurt you." If you can use the fact that you are destitute to evoke pity and sympathy, you can cover up the fact that were it not for this temporary financial setback, you would be cleaning up.

So hang in there and stay alive. (The key word is "alive"!) If you've got good properties but are caught in a cash bind, swallow your pride and talk your way out of bankruptcy. You'll be surprised at how successful you can be. After it works, stop and think again about the beauty of bankruptcy. In how many other situations could you talk someone else into paying your debts for you?

CHAPTER 12 SUMMARY

   I. Bankrupting to acquire properties.
  II. Bankruptcy creates bargains.
 III. Two interpretations of the bankruptcy rules.
 IV. Bankruptcy psychology.
  V. Poor sportsmanship in bankruptcy.
 VI. Picking up bargains:

Long-Term Property vs. Short-Term Cash

You heave a sigh of relief. "It's about time someone landed on my Oranges. I've put every penny I own into building them up. Let me look here. Three houses . . . that's $550!"

Things are looking up at last! No more complicated and risky investment decisions! All you needed was some cash for a reserve fund, and now you're in great shape. What could be simpler?

At this point, let's introduce one small complication into your rosy picture. Suppose Kim has just landed on your Oranges. But Kim doesn't want to pay that $550, and instead offers you a property if you'll agree to let her off scot-free. She has enough money to pay the rent in cash if she has to, but she'd rather make your life complicated. You must now make one of the hardest decisions which you will ever face over a Monopoly board. Should you take the property with its long-term benefits, or should you go ahead and demand payment in cash? This chapter should help you decide.

The general rule in such a situation is:
UNLESS YOU NEED THE MONEY DESPERATELY FOR SOME SHORT-TERM USE, YOU SHOULD PROBABLY TAKE THE PROPERTY.

Unfortunately, this rule has many exceptions and requires a good deal of clarification. Let's examine the important points in determining how a specific situation fits into the general rule:

1. The type of property referred to in the rule is always a color group property.

2. The first question you should ask yourself in such a situation is, "How badly do I need the cash?" If you really don't need it that badly and you could use the property, then you should definitely take the property. Even if you can't use the property right away, one of your opponents could probably use it against you if he owned it. If this is true, take the property and quietly mumble that you have no idea why you're taking a property instead of the cash, since the property is of no real use to you. If you have plenty of money, it's a good idea to pick up as many properties as you can, especially if they're being sold at reasonable prices.

3. Before you reach out and snatch up the property that he is offering, check to see whether making your opponent pay cash will force him to sell houses or otherwise severely damage his position. If he can afford to pay, then don't hesitate if you've decided to take the property. If it might be possible to make him sell those houses, think for a bit about whether it might not be worth your while to see those houses or hotels come tumbling down. But be careful. If demanding the rent in cash might force your debtor into making a trade with another opponent—a trade which could really hurt you —then don't make him mad! Take the property.

4. If you *do* need the cash, then you've got a complex decision to make. You have to balance the true value of that cash at this very moment against the value of the property, being sure to consider your chances of ever getting that property again. If it looks as if you'll get another shot at the property in the near future, there is no reason to jeopardize your position. Take the cash! If you must take a risk, make sure that the potential gain justifies that risk. If you already have a strong position, do not expose yoursef to the possibility of quick ruin for only a chance to win faster. Be patient, not greedy!

5. Suppose you are offered a property that you need desperately or that you do not think you will have anoth-

er chance of acquiring so cheaply. In this case, the small factors matter greatly:

a. Is your token in such a position that you are about to land on his expensive color group? Would a land there destroy you? If so, you'd better take the cash and hope you get another chance at that property later.

b. Is it more likely that another player will land on your property soon enough so that you won't have to survive too long without cash if you take the property now? If you see a fairly secure chance to make up the money in the near future, then take the property.

c. If you took the property now, do you have enough money and are the houses available for you to put it to immediate use? If your opponent sold that property to another player, could he use it against you immediately? If the answer to either of these questions is "yes," then take the property and cross your fingers.

This completes our brief review of the question, "Which should I take?" Although the question is no less complicated now than it was at the start of this chapter, you should have a better idea of the things to consider when choosing a correct answer.

CHAPTER 13 SUMMARY

I. Property is generally better than money.
II. How much cash is needed?
III. Another chance at the property?
IV. Another chance at the money?

Instant Cash — or Your Money Back!

Up to this point, we have been stressing the importance of property as the key to the game. However, there are times during the game when all the property in the world couldn't pull you out of a mess. Sometimes there is no substitute for good, hard Monopoly cash. How do you get it when you need it? You have a great many resources at your disposal, probably more than you realize. This chapter will discuss how to capitalize on those resources to raise whatever cash you need, at a minimal risk to your position.

"How independently can I get it?" and "How fast do I need it?" are the two questions involved in understanding how easily you can raise money. We will consider them one at a time.

How independently you can raise cash at any given moment is called the *liquidity* of your position. All of your possessions and powers in the game are called *assets*. Your assets include your properties and money and also such nonphysical quantities as the power to sell options and free lands. Any asset which you possess may be classified as either a *fixed asset* or a *liquid asset*. Liquid assets either are cash or may be turned into cash at any moment, independently of the other players in the game and without a substantial penalty. They are the real measure of how *independently* you can raise cash. Your money is a liquid asset, as are your unmortgaged properties. Your unmortgaged properties are liquid assets because they may be mortgaged and turned into cash at any time. (Technically, the Bank must charge a 10% penalty when you unmortgage a property, but this penalty is usually insignificant.)

Your houses are an example of fixed assets. True, they can be turned into cash at any time, but only by paying a 50% penalty. Mortgaged properties are also fixed assets, since the only way they can be turned into cash is through a trade or a sale to another player. Therefore, the value of those properties is *dependent* on the conditions of supply and demand in the rest of the game.

As you can see, how independently you can raise your money is really just the answer to the question, "Can I turn my assets into cash whenever I want to?" Your liquid assets are a good estimation of how much cash is easily at your disposal at any moment. To estimate your liquid assets, count up your cash on hand and add the mortgage value of all properties which are not part of complete color groups which have houses built on them. You should never have any qualms about turning these liquid assets into cash.

The question "How fast do I need it?" is a measure of how much time pressure you are under to raise the cash. If you do not need much money right away, the fact that you need a lot of money which you can't raise from just your liquid assets is slightly less painful to accept. Similarly, if you don't need to raise much money, the fact that it is needed right away is irrelevant.

There are three situations in a Monopoly game which require expenditures of large quantities of your precious money:

1. The developmental buying period, when you spend large sums of money to purchase properties from the Bank.

2. The building period, when you buy houses as quickly as is reasonable, in order to reach the critical level on your color group.

3. The unfortunate times when you land on your op-

ponents' color groups and owe large amounts of rent.

It is important to understand the similarities and differences between these periods of the game, and to understand how these can affect the way in which you choose to raise money.

The first situation in which you need money (the developmental buying period) is really not a major concern. Since you start each game with $1500, you will usually be able to buy every property you land on without much difficulty. Clearly, the money to buy these properties early in the game can be raised easily and quickly by transforming liquid assets into cash. Since these expenses come in bits and pieces, you will find that even if you are temporarily short of cash on hand to buy a property, you can get plenty of money by mortgaging one or two other properties.

When trying to build houses or pay your opponents rent, however, you will often need much larger amounts of cash. But raising the cash for building and raising the cash to pay rents, even though they both require large amounts, differ in the answers to the questions of "How independently?" and "How fast?"

When financing building on your first color group, you will probably have no substantial source of income to help you raise the money. Since this is your first color group, you have yet to collect any sizable rents. Your only important income has been the $200 which you have collected each time you passed Go. Therefore, it is usually necessary to invest most of your liquid assets in order to pay for your first building campaign. You should spend as much of your liquid assets as is necessary to reach the critical level. This often means that it is necessary to mortgage quite a few of your properties to pay for the houses. How risky is this? It's not very risky if there are no other well-developed color groups on the board and you don't need much of a cash cushion for emergencies. If there *are* other well-developed color groups, then you are in trouble, even if you don't take the risk. So build heavily and aim for that all-important critical level, even if you temporarily reduce your cash cushion to nothing.

When you need money to pay a large rent, the game will probably be a good deal "older," so there will be much more money circulating among the players. However, there will also be a *time pressure* which you rarely find when building. The game will not continue until you come up with the cash. There is no way to stall until you pass Go again, a tactic you could use when buying houses. For this reason, it is necessary to get money *faster* when paying rent.

Getting money fast often brings on many new problems. Let's examine an example from the real world. Suppose you own a shoe store. During most of the year, you are under very little time pressure to make sales (you don't eat much), so you can sell your shoes at whatever price you think they're worth. You receive a fairly steady stream of income, a supply of *money which is not too hard to get*. For every $20 you need, you have to give up (sell) only one pair of shoes.

But suppose that someone gets hurt in your store, sues you, and wins. Your insurance policy, it turns out, does not cover your situation, and you are forced to pay a lot of money. In this situation, you need to raise *a lot of money, fast!* You need to drastically increase your sales in order to get cash quickly, so you hold a big sale to try to get more customers to buy your shoes right away. You advertise that everything in the store is on sale at 50% off. Your customers know a bargain when they see one, and buy a lot more shoes than they normally would. Even at 50% off, you are still making enough profit to raise the cash you need, and you raise it faster than you normally would have. But that money was very hard to get!! For every $20 you acquired, you had to give up *two pairs of shoes,* instead of only one pair as before. You were forced to give up more of your fixed assets (the shoes) to get the money more quickly.

WHEN YOU NEED A LARGE SUM OF MONEY QUICKLY, YOU HAVE TO GIVE UP MORE OF YOUR FIXED ASSETS THAN YOU NORMALLY

WOULD TO GET THE SAME AMOUNT OF MONEY.

In a Monopoly game, the same principle applies. If you need money fast, you will not be in a very strong bargaining position to get that money. Just as in the example of the shoe store, any time you need to raise money quickly to pay a debt, you will have to keep lowering the prices until someone is willing to buy whatever it is that you are offering. Raising money to pay rents can therefore be very expensive. The same property which one of your opponents might have been willing to pay $600 for last turn might bring only $400 if you try to sell it now.

In summation, although there is a lot more money in circulation among the players when you are paying large rents, your opponents will always attempt to take advantage of your predicament and force you to give up more of your fixed assets to gain some of that available money.

With this theory in mind, you are now ready to consider the practical matter of getting money that you don't have. There are two types of items that a player can try to sell to raise money—tangible and intangible. Tangible items are physical realities, such as houses and properties. Whenever a property is sold to another player or a house is sold back to the Bank, a tangible item is being traded. On the other hand, intangible items are private agreements and promises—basically items which can't be physically held. Options, free lands, and the like are intangible items which can be sold.

Why all this talk of tangible and intangible items? The reason is what is known as the general principle of fund raising:

ALWAYS TRY TO OBTAIN CASH BY SELLING INTANGIBLE ITEMS, KNOWING THAT IF THIS FAILS, TANGIBLE PROPERTIES AND HOUSES CAN ALWAYS BE SOLD.

Translating the theory into practice is easy. Whenever

you need money in a Monopoly game, you should proceed basically as follows:

1. Mentally (without moving your lips) figure out how much money you could raise if you converted all your liquid assets into cash. Is that enough to pay your debt? If it is, heave a sigh of relief and continue, knowing that if you are unable to make a fair or profitable sale, you can always turn all your liquid assets into cash and pay the debt.

2. Now go to work on your fixed assets: try selling your intangible items to other players. Selling a free land or an option is not nearly so painful as parting with a property or selling houses for half price. Your private arrangement with other players can not be used against you in ways which you hadn't planned. A traded property can.

3. As a last resort, if you're still stuck for cash, it looks like you'll have to part with some of your valuable tangible items. If possible, maybe you can reduce your tangible losses by compromising—selling some intangibles and tangibles together. For instance, you might sell another player a free land along with a Railroad to get the money you need.

In a Monopoly game, there are six items which are commonly sold or traded between players. Other things can be traded or sold in emergencies (see Chapter 15), but these are the items which are most often put on the auction block:

1. Property. The best and the worst ways to raise money both employ property. Mortgaging your properties is the fastest and safest way to raise cash. The money is a loan from the Bank. In return for that money, you forfeit the right to collect rent on that property until you return the mortgage money along with a 10% surcharge. Otherwise, you retain all rights regarding that property. Mortgaging costs you almost nothing, since you may mortgage only properties which have no houses on them, and properties without houses collect very small rents. In addition, you may still sell or trade that property to other players as you desire. Because it is so easy and painless to mortgage and unmortgage properties, they are highly liquid assets.

Beyond the power to mortgage, however, property becomes a highly fixed asset. Although it is usually easy to raise money by selling property to another player, the amount of money which you can raise is strictly dependent on the whims and desires of the other players in the game. You can never raise any more than the conditions of supply and demand will allow, and if you are forced into selling property to raise cash when you're in trouble, you will usually receive a good deal less. Worse still is the fact that once you sell a property, the transaction is essentially irreversible. When you mortgage a property to meet a financial emergency, you can always unmortgage that property at some future time. Not so when you sell a property! Once you sell it, it is almost a certainty that you will have to pay quite a bit more to get it back, if you can get it back at all! The person who buys your property probably wants to use it or trade it to another player, and he has no intention of selling it back to you at the bargain price he paid for it. It is plain to see that the outright sale of property should be one of your last resorts when you try to raise cash.

If you find that you absolutely *must* sell property to raise money, here are some helpful hints:

a. Estimate the cheapest property that will give you enough to pay your debt and try to sell that property first. Never ask, "Does anybody want to buy one of my properties?" You would only show your opponents how desperate you really are and make bargaining that much more difficult.

b. The property you sell will probably complete a color group (such property is called a *completing property*) for one of your opponents. That is probably the only way anyone will be willing to pay much money to a person who needs money badly. If there is a housing shortage, *do not mention that fact to anyone*. Players will be very reluctant to buy a completing property if they know *in advance* that they will not be able to build on the new color group. If they do not realize that a housing shortage exists, your property becomes that much more valuable. (There is nothing ruthless about not pointing out things which it is each player's responsibility to keep track of.) However, if they do realize that there is a housing shortage, then play down the importance of quick building and stress the long-term benefits of owning a second or third color group. (Remember that a player can never bypass a housing shortage and build straight to hotels. Point out this fact if it is necessary, but only *after* you have completed the sale.)

c. When selling a property that will complete a color group for one player, keep in mind that the property has a defensive value for the other players in the game. For this reason, those players might be willing to pay a high price to keep that property from completing an opponent's color group. But before you trade a completing property to a player who is acquiring the property for purely defensive purposes, you must be confident that he will *not* make any trade with the owner of the other two properties, and he is willing to pay a reasonable amount of money. Stress the "common enemy" status of the owner of the rest of the color group and the importance of keeping that completing property away from him. If, however, you think that there is any chance that the player you sell to will turn around and trade with the common enemy, then it is much better for you to deal directly with the player who owns the rest of the color group. After all, if a partnership is going to be formed and you know you can't be the owner, being the partner is better than nothing.

d. If you end up selling a property to an opponent who owns the rest of that property's color group, insist that in addition to whatever money he pays you, he give you at least immunity on that color group. If he absolutely refuses (even after you "plead" that giving you immunity would be an act of compassion), then try to settle for two or three free lands. Ideally, you might be able to work out an immunity and half-revenues deal, especially if you phrase things in terms of a trade instead of a sale. True, you won't be able to enjoy all the big advantages of ownership, but you'll be a lot better off than you would be if you sold the property for only cash.

2. Options. Options are one of the riskier ways to raise cash, but they are still quite acceptable. Once players have seen options work, they become interested in buying, as well as selling, them. If you sell an option, you are betting that someone else will land on the property before you do. You can stress the excitement factor when you emphasize the value of the option which you are selling, and you can explain how this will add life to the game. Players who have only recently been introduced to options have a tendency to overvalue them, so try to sell your options at high prices. Start the bidding high, just don't start it so high that you will never be able to buy an option yourself in the future. A fair range for buying and selling options is about $300—600. Remember that the true value of an option is determined by supply and demand. Don't get carried away with selling your options, however. Selling your option means that you will never be able to acquire that property without trading or bankrupting. In addition, options become a less viable way of raising money as the game progresses, as fewer and fewer properties remain unowned.

3. Free passes. These are handy devices to sell when you need cash, but not too much of it. If a player is in good position to land on your color group, it is never a bad idea to offer to sell a free pass, unless you need to bankrupt or severely damage that player's position. A lot of people like this kind of quick "flight insurance," and this guarantees that you will receive some money, no matter how badly the dice treat you. Often, after one player has bought a free pass and then landed on your color group, other players will want to take advantage of the same offer. Why not? Sell all the free passes you can if the price is right.

4. Free lands. If you have a color group developed to the critical level, free lands are relatively easy to peddle. But beware! By selling a free land, you are forfeiting a part of your future rent, as well as any immediate chance of bankrupting your customer. Sell free lands as selectively as possible. Usually the best time to sell free lands is when you have two developed color groups. Then you always have a second way to collect money from your customers, even if you sell free lands on your more important color group.

The most likely target for your sales of free lands is the one who can least afford to land on your properties. But although he may be your most eager customer, it may not be your most intelligent move to sell him a free land. After all, bankrupting power and the power to severely weaken an opponent's position can be very important powers. Don't let them go without giving considerable thought to what you are sacrificing. If you feel that it is worthwhile to get the money now, keep two things in mind as you try to sell your free lands:

a. When you must raise cash to avoid selling houses, free lands sell very poorly. This is because any potential customers know that if they can't buy your free lands, you will probably be forced to sell houses on those same properties on which they would be buying free lands. If you are forced to sell below the critical level, that's almost as good as a free land! You might try to counter this reasoning by saying that it is to their advantage to see those houses stay up if they're not paying on them, since this would help to weaken the positions of the other players in the game.

b. When you sell a player a free land, you take away his need to keep a cushion of money to guard against the possibility of landing on your color group. Where will this player invest the funds which he was saving to pay you? Be careful not to contribute to your own demise!

5. Percentages of future cash revenues. If you have a color group all to yourself (no partners), this can be a good way to raise money. Percentages of revenues are usually sold in blocks of 25%, but any percentage agreeable to both parties in the sale is fine. If your color group is well developed, you should find plenty of other players who are willing to cash in on your success. Try to sell your promise of a percentage of future revenues to one of your weaker opponents. In that manner, when that player goes bankrupt, you will regain your rights to all of the profits from your color group.

Also emphasize in your negotiations that a player who buys one-fourth of the future cash revenues in your color group is entitled to a 25% discount whenever he lands on that color group.

Percentages of revenues which you have *already sold* can help you in times of financial hardship. If you are about to be forced to sell houses on a color group in which another player has an interest, he will be much more likely to bail you out. Who wants 25 or 50% of the rent collected on Illinois Avenue if that rent is only $20?

Watch out for a trap which can be set by a player who owns two (or more) color groups and offers to sell quarters of future cash revenues. If he has developed the cheaper color group to the critical level and has kept the more expensive color group without houses, he might sell 75 or even 100% of his anticipated future cash revenues on the cheaper color group and use the money he got from selling his quarters of future revenues to develop his more expensive color group to the critical level. Finally, he can trade the cheaper color group to another player, and everyone who was originally promised a percentage of the revenues is left with nothing. One hundred percent of nothing is still nothing, so buy percentages of your opponents' future revenues with caution—this trick is a common snare among ruthless players.

6. *Immunity*. In most cases, immunity is a bad thing to sell. Selling immunity is in many ways like selling property. Immunity is a permanent promise; once it is given, it cannot be withdrawn. You forfeit your chance to ever use that color group to bankrupt the player whom you give immunity. This usually means that if you don't have a second way of bankrupting that person, you will find yourself in trouble in the long run.

Do not sell immunity cheaply. However, if by selling immunity you can accomplish an important goal, you should be able to bankrupt some third player at some time in the future and use his color group against your immune opponent. Immunity is often traded for another immunity or is offered as part of a trade which could not be completed without it.

There are times when it is an excellent idea to try to sell immunity. Immunity is a private arrangement and is destroyed whenever the properties are traded. Thus, the best time to sell immunity is right before you trade away your color group! But make sure that you don't sell immunity and then discover that you are unable to complete the trade. Once you are reasonably certain that you can swap an entire color group with someone else, it becomes reasonable for you to trade or sell immunities. Make certain that the player who receives immunity from you is aware that it is a private arrangement and is conditional upon your ownership of the color group. If necessary, you can reassure him that you would not want to lose all the money which you invested in houses by selling them at half price. Then, when the time is ripe, tear 'em down and trade. *(Note: this might tend to hurt your credibility.)* You might have to trade down in profit-earning power, but all the immunities will be gone and you can use all the money you gained to build heavily on your new color group.

These are the six most easily and commonly sold items for raising cash when you need it. Mr. Expert makes good use of all the tangible and intangible resources which his position provides. But sometimes everything fails! When this happens, it is time to call out the emergency reserve of ideas. The next chapter will deal with the offbeat and humorous tactics which are used by desperate players. They won't all work, and the ones that work won't work all the time, but if you can pull one of them off, you will have demonstrated the ex-

pert's ability to get more out of his position than is really
in it.

CHAPTER 14 SUMMARY

I. "How independently?" and "How fast?"
II. Liquid assets vs. fixed assets.
III. The three situations which require money.
IV. Tangible and intangible items.
V. The general principle of fund raising.
VI. The six things commonly sold:
   A. Property.
   B. Options.
   C. Free passes.
   D. Free lands
   E. Revenue sharing.
   F. Immunity.

Apparent Insanity for Fun and Profit

There is something funny about the way a desperate player will act to avoid bankruptcy. The threat of losing the game seems to bring out the creativity and imagination in many people. After all, since it's only a game, why not try a really way-out deal? If every other player in the game is willing to go along with it, what's the difference?

We have collected a sampling of some of the zaniest, wackiest, but still useful ideas that we have seen. If you find yourself in a real bind, why not try to use one or two of them? You can hide your desperation behind your laughter, and who knows? Maybe one of the fish will bite! Don't be afraid to use your own imagination to save your real estate empire. They laughed at some of Rockefeller's ideas too!

The first idea can work if one of your opponents is getting really frustrated by a housing shortage. If that's the case and you need some money, tell him that for the right fee you'll be happy to (*a*) build a hotel on one property of a color group which has four houses on each property already, thus releasing four houses onto the market, or (*b*) sell houses back to the Bank from one of your cheaper color groups. If the other player has plenty of cash and nothing to spend it on, he might be willing to pay you a very tidy sum to make houses available. Remember: it is illegal to sell or transfer houses between players. You can only promise to return houses to the Bank.

Selling free passes and free lands is just like selling insurance, right? Why not really go all out in opening up your very own insurance company? Offer to insure anything if you're paid enough. Insure your opponents against ever having to pay $50 to get out of Jail again? Why not? Let your imagination run wild!

Options bring out the gambling nature in players, so be blatant and offer to gamble if you need the money badly enough. The rules never prohibit gambling, and since you're not using real money, the local authorities should have no objection. If you need some cash, why not bet a friend a $100 bill that he can't roll a higher number on one die than you can? If you're in trouble, what've you got to lose?

This next trick is a real beauty. A friend of ours once saved a game using this one. He landed on another player's hotel and was in big trouble. After scrounging and selling, he was $30 short. With a wild, desperate look in his eyes, he asked us if there was any objection to his making up the difference with money *from his own wallet!* We knew that he didn't like to lose, but this was definitely a first. We finally decided that anyone who was that devoted deserved a chance to pay in real cash, so we reluctantly agreed. Sure enough, he took out his wallet and pulled $30 . . . *in Monopoly money!* He had come to the game with a wallet full of Monopoly money, just to trap us on a sucker's proposition.

If you play with a jackpot in the game (usually consisting of money collected from various taxes, assessments, and other fines, and often an additional $500 from the Bank), this trick can net you a good amount from the gamblers in the game. If you are on the street before Free Parking, why not offer to sell your next turn? For a fee, a player could buy whatever happened to you on your next throw of the dice. If the board is built up with lots of hotels, you could use the same idea, only reversed. You could agree to absorb any penalties which your customer incurred on his next throw of the dice. The effect would be similar to that of selling him a free pass on your own color group, except you'd be obligated to pay (instead of waive) a debt. *Caution*: if you guarantee to pay him enough money to cover any debt and then find that you can't raise the money, you are *bankrupt* to him, so watch out for Chance squares which might present him with an unexpected "Advance to Boardwalk." Finally, you could offer to buy the rent collection privilege on another player's color group for one turn. For a fee to the owner, you would be entitled to collect all rents on that property during that turn. (Frankly, it's no more than a lease.)

You could even take the previous ploy one step further. You could sell your rights to the jackpot. For a large sum of money now, you could promise that if you are the next player to land on Free Parking, you will turn over all the cash you collect from the jackpot to the person who buys your option. If there is enough money in the jackpot, selling those rights can bring in a hefty chunk of cash.

This gambit is pushing it a bit, but if you laugh enough, it can net you a few dollars. If the game is being played at your house, open a little store! "Sell" drinks and refreshments, liquor, and cigarettes. Since most players will refuse to pay their Monopoly money directly to you, have them pay it into the jackpot. That will make the pot sweeter—with their money! If you happen to land there, you deserve it. After all, it was your idea!

This next ploy is a dirty trick and really should be avoided unless you are playing against your worst enemies. If you're willing to tolerate screams and threats, then the next time you sell or trade a property to someone else, mortgage it before you transfer it to close the deal. Do this very quietly, and if your opponent asks you when you mortgaged it, begin to count your money very intently and to whistle "Home on the Range." This maneuver is a very painful way to pick up a few extra dollars, but some players use it. Watch out for opponents who do!

This trick is complicated and almost impossible to use successfully, but if you're well coordinated and a smooth talker, it can net you a couple of dollars in time of desperation. Take one of your utilities or Railroads (never risk a color property) and ask if anyone wants to buy it at any price. If nobody wants to buy it, mortgage it and then toss it into the Bank. Announce that the Bank is auctioning off this property, that nobody is interested in buying it, and that you will buy it for $10. Sold! By this time, your opponents will all be staring at you, wondering what you think you're doing with these shady maneuvers. Now, here's the trick: when you bought the property at auction from the Bank, you bought it unmortgaged! Now, mortgage it a second time and collect your mortgage money again. This shouldn't work and rarely will, but you never know . . .

The final cash-raising tactic is the most difficult to pull off, but if your opponents have been drinking heavily, it just might work. Announce that you are setting up . . . (are you ready?) . . . a Legal Defense Fund! Declare that any contributions made to your defense fund are totally tax-deductible. Any such contribution may be deducted from whatever they are forced to pay when they draw a Chance card assessing a Poor Tax, a Community Chest card assessing a School Tax, or when they land on the Luxury Tax or Income Tax squares. Maybe your inebriated opponents would rather pay you now and deduct the expense at tax time.

We make no claims for the legality of any of these gimmicks to save you from disaster. However, if you can use your negotiating skill to convince the other players in the game to permit you to use them, more power to you!

Here are some unusual strategies which don't apply to quick raising of money. Rather, they have a more general effect of adding crazy nuances to your game:

1. Try to go first! It may seem unimportant, but the player who goes first has an edge over the other players, especially the player who goes last. The first player has very little chance of landing on properties which have already been bought during his entire first trip around the board. He has first crack at every color group he can get to. By the time the third and fourth players roll the dice, several other players have already trampled over some of the best properties.

So what can you do if you have the bad luck to roll a low number before the game and appear doomed to go last? Why not offer the guy who rolled the highest number $100 to switch places with you? The right to go first is worth at least $100, so why not try to buy it? In some college tournaments, players place sealed bids to determine who goes first. One player decided that going first was such an advantage that he bid a record $225 for the privilege. He even won the game! So don't feel foolish offering $50 or $100 for that precious first roll.

2. Everyone knows that a "Get out of Jail Free" card is worth $50 (the cost of paying your way out of Jail), right? Guess again! A "Get out of Jail Free" card is worth whatever another player is willing to pay for it. This card has a very important use other than as the traditional key to the Jail. It is often used as a *cash transfer device*.

Suppose you want to loan a player $500. The rules officially outlaw all loans, so you simply buy his "Get out of Jail Free" card for $500. When he has enough money to pay you back, he can buy the card back from you for $500. The rules say that the owner of the "Get out of Jail Free" card can sell it for whatever he can get. In fighting a balance-of-power battle, it can be an indispensible weapon. What happens if *you* own the "Get out of Jail Free" card when you want to loan another player money? Sell it to him for $1 and buy it back for $501! The "Get out of Jail Free" card was used for that very purpose in the last World Monopoly Championships.

What does this mean as far as the value of the "Get out of Jail Free" card is concerned? It means that if your opponent draws such a card, it would be a good idea to offer him $70 for it. He'll look at you as if you're some sort of a nut, but just smile. If he hesitates, offer him $80. As you can see, they can be handy little cards, and even if you don't have to use it as a cash transfer device, it's well worth the extra $30 to watch your opponents go up a wall trying to figure out what you could possibly do with the card to make it worth any more than $50.

3. This next maneuver is commonly referred to as the Abby Normal strategy. It's a real zinger! The method of this strategy is never to collect any of the petty rents—the ones under $30. This strategy is widely used by many tournament players, even though it might at first appear totally insane not to collect money owed to you, no matter how small. Here are some of the major benefits of this strategy:

a. If you don't collect the small rents, maybe your opponents won't either. In that case, Monopoly games go much quicker, since the players no longer have to count out those pesky little $14 rents. In fact, if everyone agrees not to collect rents under $30, you can stop using $1 and $5 bills and round everything off to the nearest $10. You'll find that if everyone stops collecting the little rents, it will all even out in the long run. It's the big rents that make the difference.

b. If your opponents continue to collect all the petty rents, they will start to feel very cheap. This is especially true when you explain that the reason you're not collecting the rents is to help the game move faster so that *everyone* will benefit.

c. Even if your opponents still continue to collect the little ones, it will be very easy for you to convince them that you either are crazy or are employing a secret strategy. This can make the game a lot more fun for you. Mix them up even more and only collect even-numbered rents or rents that are divisible by 7! Better still, don't collect small rents until someone lands on your Mediterranean Avenue. Then make a big fuss and insist on receiving your mighty $2. If you want a real treat, watch your opponents' faces.

The Abby Normal strategy may seem a bit weird, but it can really make the game entertaining for you. And stranger things have been known to pay off.

4. Earlier in this book, you met Gary, a true worshipper of the Green group. Now we introduce his sister Karen, and what is affectionately known as the Karen Joy strategy. The idea behind this ploy is to completely confuse your opponents. Pretend that you've fallen in love with a different color group every few turns. This will keep them totally in the dark as to the color group you are really after. (This strategy can even be used if you're not really sure which one you're really after.) Every few turns, make some comment about this or that color group being the absolute *best* and the one that you would really love to have. The trick is to be completely sincere when you talk in praise of each color group. Your opponents will be completely unable to fathom how you can possibly change your mind so often. Stay sincere and keep your opponents guessing! This way, it will be very easy to acquire the color group you are really after.

5. Or how about the old Blue Chips maneuver? At the start of the game, announce that your pet lion has eaten all of the Monopoly money. Explain that you have substituted poker chips for the missing money. If your

opponents have never played poker before, then you're in great shape. After all, if everyone is confused as to the true value of their money, an enterprising young guy could do very well for himself. Just think . . .

This concludes the introduction to the humorous, desperate side of Monopoly games. The next time things start getting dull, why not put some life into things? There is no reason why you shouldn't enjoy yourself while methodically crushing your opponents!

CHAPTER 15 SUMMARY

    I. Get paid to release houses.
   II. Insurance company.
  III. Gambling.
  IV. Monopoly money in the wallet.
   V. Jackpot insurance.
  VI. Sales jackpot rights.
 VII. Refreshments.
VIII. Quick mortgaging.
  IX. Mortgage–auction–mortgage.
   X. Legal Defense Fund.
  XI. "Get out of Jail Free" card play.
 XII. Abby Normal strategy.
XIII. Karen Joy strategy.
XIV. Blue Chips maneuver.

"The Brooklyn Bridge Is a Bargain"

Have you ever been talked into buying something that you really didn't need? If you haven't, you're a rare exception in today's society. In this modern, complex world, a good deal of time, effort, and money is constantly being spent in trying to influence people's decision-making processes. Entire industries, such as TV and radio, depend on the money they receive from advertisers who believe that commercials will increase the sales of their products. The art of convincing people can sometimes seem more like a science. Is it possible to apply some of that science to a Monopoly game? We can try.

Common sense dictates that in any capitalistic economy people will always act to safeguard *what they perceive as their best interests*. In addition, one of the principal complaints about a free-market economy is that people think only in terms of their short-term interests, neglecting the long-term effects of their actions (for example, people want cars, but don't care about pollution). These two weaknesses can be exploited when influencing the actions of opponents. Simply, whenever we negotiate, we should try to:

CHANGE OUR OPPONENT'S PERCEPTION OF HIS OWN BEST INTERESTS.

APPEAL TO HIS SHORT-SIGHTED NATURE.

No matter how seriously you may want to win, a Monopoly game is only a game. For this reason, many of the methods used to influence people in the real world will not work. Your opponents realize that the worst thing that can happen to them in a game is that (horrors!) they might lose. For this reason, tactics like direct physical coercion are clearly ineffective—your opponent will just stand up and leave. You're wasting your breath if you try to convince your baby sister or disinterested boyfriend that "it's not really in your best interests to charge me that $1100 rent." If you want to play to win, you will have to accept the fact that people who are playing only to have a good time will not be thinking in the same way that you do. If you don't realize this, Monopoly can be a very frustrating experience. When a good player tries to make a highly complex trade in a game which is geared toward simple, unsophisticated strategies, he is making a severe mistake. The first rule of trading is:

TAILOR YOUR STRATEGY TO THE GAME AT HAND.

Do not try to introduce the more advanced concepts into a game where they are unnecessary to ensure your victory or where they would be clearly out of place. There is no need to overpower and confuse your opponents with your knowledge. If you are engaged in a nice, easygoing Monopoly game, your general knowledge of investment timing and trading should be more than enough to win.

If you are a tennis champion playing with your eight-year-old brother, you do not need to serve aces and smash lobs in order to win the game. Solid, steady playing will keep you on top. If in a Monopoly game things start looking dangerous, then it might be the time to bring in an option or a simple revenue-sharing agreement. Try to keep as many tricks up your sleeve as you possibly can.

But a Monopoly game is not a typical game. For some inexplicable reason, some players try to win with a passion and zeal that exceeds that found in their daily working life. Some players, viewing their jobs as frustrating, see the game as an escape into the high-finance world of real estate development and trading. These players are much more susceptible to arguments you may make about their own "self-interest" in the game. This leads to the second rule of trading:

THE MORE YOUR OPPONENTS CARE ABOUT WINNING, THE MORE EASILY INFLUENCED THEY WILL BE.

Suppose you find yourself in a real cutthroat game. Everyone cares about winning and losing, and nobody wants to make a bad deal. To beat these opponents, you will need more than your knowledge of investments and timing—they probably have the same knowledge. You will have to convince them to make deals which are better for you than they are for them. Not only will a good trader get the better end of the deal, he will also be able to do so without letting his opponent know it (at least not until it's too late to do anything about it). In fact, a really shrewd trader will make his opponent believe that he has robbed the trader blind. In any case, you want your opponent to believe that he has gotten at least an even deal. Your goal is to make trades that make you appear to be either a fair trader or a fool.

How do you go about convincing a highly suspicious opponent that the trade you are suggesting is really fair? The first and most reliable way is to explain the deal logically, in just the manner that your opponent wants to hear it. Your verbal representation will make an important impression on the person with whom you are trading. The way you describe a trade can alter the way in which a person views the entire situation.

Here is an example of the wrong way and the right way to present a proposal:

WRONG

"Don't be a turkey. Give me that Red property and I'll build on the three Reds. I agree not to charge you rent, and to show you how nice I am, I'll even give you half the money I take in. Why should you care if I have a powerful color group, as long as I don't hurt you? And don't think that just because you're landing free, you're part owner. I can do whatever I want with those properties. Just be glad that I'm willing to put my own money into building houses that make your half revenues amount to something. Okay?"

RIGHT

"Why don't we become partners? Together we can do very well for ourselves and wipe these other guys out early. If we combine your third Red property with the two Reds that I have (or, If we combine your two Red properties with my third one and my money), then we would have a color group which could bring us a lot of income. I would be willing to pay for all the building costs and act as owner of the property. However, you would be completely immune from ever paying me rent on those properties, and of course, we would split any cash revenues I collect 50–50. If I invest some money and property and you throw in your property, we could start collecting a lot of money as soon as the other players start landing there. Then, after all the other players get wiped out, I'd tear everything down, since I can't possibly hurt you on *our* color group! Is it a deal?"

This rather obvious contrast displays both of the important trading principles clearly. You change your opponent's perception of you from a hostile enemy to an opponent with whom he can profitably cooperate until it becomes time to part ways. You point out the advantages clearly and admit that the deal would be profitable for both of you. You also encourage and exploit your opponent's shortsightedness by emphasizing the possibilities for immediate profits. You do *not* mention your long-term advantage of bankrupting power or your right to trade the color group away. Finally, you allay any fears which he might have by explaining that when you and your partner are the only players left in the game, the color group will become worthless.

In a simple trade which appears fair on the surface, a

clear, logical presentation which stresses advantages for both sides and which follows the two guidelines presented at the beginning of the chapter should prove quite convincing—even to your most doubtful opponent.

The trade you want to offer is not always so nice, however. Suppose the deal you want to propose is so blatantly unfair that if you were to explain it clearly, your opponent would instantly refuse. In such a case, it is necessary to convince your opponent that whatever you are offering him is far more valuable than it really is. You need to bluff a Monopoly player in the same way that an experienced poker player can bluff in a high-stakes poker game.

To bluff well in a Monopoly game, you need three attributes:

1. Sincerity. This can't be learned, but you can fake it with practice.

2. A superior knowledge of the true value of those items which you are trading. You already have this.

3. The ability to successfully confuse your opponent. By continuously bombarding your opponent with new proposals, irrelevant facts, and "evidence" of the fairness of your proposal, you never give your opponent a chance to see why the deal you are suggesting is really unfair. The rest of this chapter will deal with this attribute.

Here is an example of a bluffer in action:

Evelyn	*Liz*
3 Railroads	1 Railroad
1 Utility	1 Utility
1 Red property	2 Red properties

Liz has been trying to get the third Red property from Evelyn, and she's about to try again.

LIZ: Listen, Evelyn, I'll give you the fourth Railroad to complete your Railroad group and I'll give you the

second utility to complete your utility group, plus
I'll even toss in some cash, if you give me your one
Red property. Your Railroads would start collect-
ing $200 right away.

EVELYN: Well . . .

LIZ: It's a fair deal—two properties and some cash for
one property.

EVELYN: Let me think about it for a while.

LIZ: No. We have to strike while the iron is hot. If you
really don't think the deal is fair, I'm willing to turn
it around—we've got to do something before Shelly
gets too powerful. How about if you give me all of
your Railroads and one utility, and I give you one
of the Red properties.

EVELYN: But I'd need your other Red property to complete the color group.

LIZ: All right. I'll give you both Reds, but to compensate
for my giving up an extra property, I'll want $500
cash and immunity on the Red color group.

EVELYN: I still don't know . . .

LIZ: Look, Ev, I've offered it to you both ways. One
way has to be better for you, so you choose which
one. You give me the Railroads, the utilities, cash,
and immunity in exchange for two of my properties,
or I give you the Railroads, the utilities, and cash
for *one* of your properties. We've got to trade now.
We can't sit here forever.

EVELYN: I think I want the two Reds.

LIZ: Great. *(She smiles.)* Give me all four of those properties, $500 cash, and don't forget—I'm immune
forever on those Reds and you keep on paying me on
the Railroads. Oh, by the way, these Red properties
are mortgaged. And I really should get a quarter
of your profits on the Reds.

EVELYN: Wait a second. I think I'll take the four Rail-
roads and the two utilities, and just give you one
Red property. By the way I want immunity on the
Red color group.

LIZ: Well, okay.

*   *   *

The bluff worked. Of course, the far better deal was to take the Red group—Liz is probably cleaning up right now. Liz never really had any intention of trading away her two Reds, but she kept pretending until she finally convinced Evelyn that it would be foolish not to take two properties and some money in exchange for one. Notice how Liz claimed that she was going to "turn the deal around," but when she reversed the offer, all sorts of new terms and conditions seemed to magically appear. This is a very common hustling tactic, and that's just what Liz is doing—hustling. She pressured Evelyn into making the trade.

It is probably a better idea to learn how to spot a hustler and protect yourself than it is to try to become one. Sometimes, however, a good bluff involving turning a trade around to a position which you would never really accept can ensure your victory, not to mention making the game much more exciting for you.

A final word on bluffing. If your opponent is smart enough to see that you are offering a ridiculous deal, he will naturally try to call your bluff if you turn it around. As soon as you realize that you will not be able to get away with this bluff, you will have to back out as politely as possible. This is most believeably done by suddenly "noticing" that your opponent has another property which you didn't think he had, or "discovering" that you have much less money than you thought you did. An offer is not binding until both parties have agreed. A player can back out of a deal at any time until both parties have decided on the terms of a final agreement, and whatever properties are involved in the trade have changed hands. There is one danger in backing out of a bluff. Once your bluff has been exposed, you will find it very difficult to bluff at any later time in the game.

At this point, it is worth devoting some discussion to the concept of a "reversible" trade. *Reversing an offer* is taking the terms of an opponent's offer and applying them in your "equivalent" counteroffer to him. For example, suppose your opponent has Boardwalk and you have Park Place. If your opponent offers to buy Park Place for $200 (he thinks you're a fool), you could reverse the offer by offering to buy Boardwalk from him for $200. When your opponent refuses, it is good strategy at this point to tell your opponent that he should only bother to offer you trades which he would accept himself. His offers will become much fairer very quickly. Reversibility is often a very good test of the fairness of a deal.

However, not all offers are reversible. Sometimes you can't offer your opponent the same thing he offers you, and sometimes the true value of a property is much higher for one player than for another. If your opponent is offering you three Railroads, you obviously can't reverse the offer and offer him three Railroads! When it is possible to reverse an offer, it is sometimes a good idea to do so, even if you would have been happy to accept that offer in the first place. Why not see what his reaction is to taking what he's offering? He might decide to make his offer even sweeter. It usually doesn't hurt to ask.

Thus, a good trader is usually a good talker, and talking trades is what separates the robber barons from the robbed bankrupts in Monopoly. Just follow the guidelines and look for your opponent's weaknesses. In most cases, if you can phrase your deal right, your opponent will gladly go along with what you're saying, even if it really destroys his position.

So suggest an option; if the opponents balk, propose a partnership. No go? Sell insurance, and if things get really sticky, create a housing shortage and drive 'em all into the streets! Here's the one game where you can destroy empires and amass fortunes without harming a single soul—except, perhaps, somebody's pride. That's the magic of it all, for novices and tournament masters alike.

See you on Boardwalk!

CHAPTER 16 SUMMARY

    I. Perception of best interests.
   II. Shortsightedness.
  III. Tailor your strategy.
  IV. How much do your opponents care about winning?
   V. Bluffing.
  VI. Reversing an offer.

How to Spot, Stop, and Top a Cheater

Up to this point we have been telling you that a Monopoly game is only a game. We're sorry. We lied. to some people it must be a life-and-death experience. Why else would people who are otherwise kind, honest, and moral decide to become criminals?

We've all felt the temptation to cheat at one time or another, but naturally we've suppressed it. But don't be so sure that your neighbor, your wife, or your mother-in-law will have the willpower that you have. The more you beat them, the more frustrated they will get. The more frustrated they get, the more likely it will become that some "accidents" might happen which were not happening before. We can't explain why, but we can explain how. That's what this chapter is for.

So here they are, the most frequently used, effective ways of cheating in a Monopoly game. Forewarned is forearmed.

1. Watch out for the player who seems to spend a large part of the game collecting his Go salary. One good explanation for why a player may seem to be collecting a lot of Go money is that he is collecting it more than once each time around the board. If a player suddenly remembers that he passed Go two turns earlier, make a mental note of it and see if he remembers "late" again later on in the game. It could be that he is remembering twice each time he passes Go! The way to prevent this is to make sure that the Banker pays players their $200 the moment that they pass or land on Go. In college

tournaments the Banker actually keeps a checklist to prevent double or forgotten payments.

2. This one is extremely difficult to prove, so watch out for the player who looks like he is about to try it. When a player buys $1100 worth of houses and throws a pile of hundreds into the Bank to pay for them, how do you know how much money he's paid? If that pile of hundreds landed on another pile of hundreds, there's almost no way to tell. The high cost of houses is a great enticement for players to try and shortchange the Bank a little (a lot?). There is usually only one sure way to stop this type of cheating. Make it a "house rule" that whenever any houses are bought, the money must be counted in the center of the board to prevent mistakes.

3. During the game, keep an eye on the Banker and how efficiently he operates. Watch for any signs that he is mixing his own money with the Bank's. Often a cheat will suddenly pull money out of the Bank, and explain, "Oh, the Bank owed me $300—I lent it some hundreds a few turns ago when it ran out." If you suspect any embezzling, maybe it's time you asked if you could try your hand at banking for a while.

4. There are quite a few cheating methods which can be categorized generally as "wrong change maneuvers." By using these, one of your opponents could be getting more than the proverbial five pennies for his nickel. (Groucho Marx always did argue for a good 7-cent nickel.) There are two outstanding methods in this category.
   a. When one player owes another player a large debt, the creditor will often ask that the debtor convert his small change to large bills. The debtor will count his money and toss it into the Bank (similar to the building cheat) and explain that the Bank now owes his creditor the required sum. This is the small change

cheat. You can stop him by insisting that no player other than the Banker ever be allowed to put or take money from the Bank. Keeping the Bank neat can also help, since it is harder for a cheat to toss his money in and immediately make it indistinguishable from the rest of the Bank's funds.

b. Sometimes, when a player passes Go, instead of collecting two one-hundred-dollar bills, he takes a five-hundred-dollar bill, muttering something to the effect of, "I'll take five hundred and pay the Bank three hundred." Make sure that when a player says that he'll pay $300, he actually does. Once again, the best way to prevent accidental $500 collections is to require that all transactions go through the Banker.

5. Do you know what the world's most widely held currency is? If you guessed "Monopoly money," you were correct. There is more Monopoly money in general circulation today than there is U.S. currency. (However, the present U.S. inflation is giving the game a "run for the money.") Here's how a cheat uses this fact to his own advantage.

Before he comes to the game, he takes a couple of one-hundred-dollar bills from his Monopoly set at home and puts them in his shirt pocket ($700 is usually a nice amount). During the game, he puts some of his cash-on-hand *into* his shirt pocket, being careful to make sure that another player notices him put it there. The other player can't be sure how much he put in, but he does notice several bills (a $100 bill on top of five $10 bills). Some time later in the game, our cheat takes a large wad of money out of his pocket. If anyone questions where this money came from, he explains that he'd saved it from earlier in the game and calls on his "witness" to document his story.

This type of cheat is pretty smart. The best way to stop such "inflation" is to require that all money be kept on the table at all times. Technically, it is prefectly legal to hide your money in your pocket or under the board, but it is considered good sportsmanship to keep your money on the table at all times and to accurately answer anyone who asks you how much cash you have. Make it a "house rule" that no money may leave the table, explaining that this will help alleviate any confusion as to who has how much money. Watch out for players who are constantly dropping their money. They may be picking up some spare cash.

6. Always be suspicious of the player who moves pieces without counting squares and also seems to have the amazing luck to miss your color group every time. Many people can move pieces without counting the squares, but it's a good idea to check their moves very carefully. Dice are very easy to misread, either accidentally or intentionally. When their mistakes are pointed out, it is also very common for these cheats to suddenly remember starting from a square quite different from the one which you remember. If you feel that this type of cheat has become a problem in your game, insist that after each roll of the dice, the roll be announced properly so that there is no confusion. The method which is most useful is to announce the number shown on the dice and the square from which the turn began. For example, if you are on Illinois Avenue and roll a seven, you would say, "Seven from Illinois." If this is done before the token is moved or the dice are picked up, many "accidents" can be prevented.

7. The next trick is a dice trick. Often when a player rolls doubles, he picks up the dice, gives just a little shake, and rolls doubles again. Most of the times this happens, it is unintentional, but every so often . . . The best thing to do is to insist that all players shake the dice well before each roll.

* * *

8. Watch out for the "It's leaning!" cheat. He's the guy who rolls a five, lands on your well-developed color group, and then suddenly notices that one of the dice is leaning against the pile of Chance cards. True, it's only leaning slightly (maybe imperceptibly), but he will demand another throw of the dice so that they will lie flat. A variation on this type of cheater is the player who rolls one dice on top of one of the piles of cards. Since there is no standard agreement as to whether this is a "good" or a "bad" roll, he quickly calculates whether or not he likes the number showing on the dice. If he does, he takes it; if he he doesn't, he declares that a dice on top of a pile of cards is obviously "bad." The way to stop this cheat is to agree at the beginning of the game (or the first time the situation occurs) what will and what will not count as fair rolls of the dice. A fairly standard agreement is that any time both dice land on the board and do not lean unreasonably the number counts.

9. The next few cheaters work with Chance and Community Chest cards. First is the one who simply misreads them. A player has to have a very good reason not to want the card he drew to take the high risk of getting caught at misreading. Usually he will save his misreading for the "Advance to Boardwalk" or "Advance to Illinois Avenue" card. In general, it's a good idea to ask each player to show all the other players the card he picks before replacing it at the bottom of the deck.

10. Another common card cheater is the one who slightly bends the corner of the deadlier cards as he reads them. In this manner, he knows when the dangerous cards are the next to come up. If he is unfortunate enough to land on the Chance square when one of these cards is on top, he suddenly becomes very clumsy and knocks the entire pile of cards across the room. What an

interesting coincidence! Keep your eye out for "marked" cards.

11. This type of cheating is employed at the start of the game. The cheater pretends to shuffle the Chance and Community Chest cards without drawing much attention to himself. He subtly puts the "Advance to Boardwalk" card on top of the deck. After play begins, if he is the first person to land on a Chance square, he gleefully draws the card and advances to Boardwalk, which he promptly buys. If another player lands on a Chance square first, he exclaims, "Did anyone cut these cards?" and quickly cuts them himself, preventing the opponent from drawing the "Advance to Boardwalk" card right away. If some other player says he saw the cheat shuffle the cards himself, he explains that he shuffled the Community Chest, but not the Chance cards. To stop this one, just make sure that the Chance and Community Chest cards are shuffled and cut in full view before every game.

12. The last type of card cheater is the "holdout cheater." He fails to return the card which he drew back to the deck. This can happen accidentally, too, so if he gets caught there isn't too much suspicion. The "holdout cheater" will drop the "bad" card on the floor or gently slide it under his properties. If it is an important enough card, this can make a very big difference in the outcome of the game. Some holdout cheaters even go so far as to remove cards before the game begins and then "find" them when they see it is to their advantage to have the card in circulation. To beat the "holdout cheater," skim through the Chance cards *before* they are shuffled at the beginning of the game and make sure that all 16 Chance cards are there. Then, once the game has begun, watch very carefully where those cards go when they are drawn.

* * *

13. Since title deed cards have a lot of numbers on them, mistakes occur fairly frequently when they are used. With some people, however, such mistakes are not always accidental. When asked how much rent is owed, this type of cheat quickly answers the rent which would be charged if there were one more house on his property. This is most likely to occur:

a. when the houses are sloppily arranged on the color group, or

b. shortly after he has sold several houses back to the Bank. The excuse here is, "Oh, I forgot I sold those back to the Bank a few turns ago!"

To stop this cheat can sometimes be slightly embarrassing. After all, it seems impolite to say, "Let me see the title deed" every time you land on an opponent's color group. The best method to prevent this type of error is to familiarize yourself with the approximate rents and to check to see how many houses are actually built on the property on which you have landed. When your opponent announces the rent, make sure it sounds reasonable. The rent shouldn't be very high if he hasn't reached the critical level. If the rent requested seems unfair, ask your creditor to double-check, stating clearly the number of houses he should be checking the rent for. If it is really an accident, the creditor will discover his mistake. If he's a cheat, this is usually enough to change his mind. But don't think he won't try it again!

One last word about proper rent collection. Remember that the last property in each color group has rents slightly higher than the other properties in the same color group. By accident, a player will often use the more expensive title deed card when computing what rent you owe. Make sure that you do not pay the rent for the more expensive property unless you land on that property. On the more expensive color groups it can make quite a difference.

14. Some players won't realize that this next maneuver is cheating. It is illegal to remain in Jail more

than three turns. The cheat will try and stay for five or six turns. Why? Because if there are a lot of color groups well-developed with houses and hotels, what safer place to be than in Jail? A person in Jail can build, collect rents, and trade, just like a person out of Jail. The only thing he can't do is pay rents to his opponents. Most players who stay in Jail too long do so by accident. It is a good idea to take three one-dollar bills, marked "1st," "2nd," and "3rd," and place them by the Jail square. Then, after each roll of the dice of a player in Jail, the next dollar bill is turned over to show how long the player has been in Jail. Remember, three strikes and you're out!

15. Watch out for the Monopoly rule creator. He claims to know every last rule and manages to have the right rule for every occasion. He is at his best when your Monopoly set is missing its copy of the rules. By now you have a thorough knowledge of all the important rules. Don't let this cheat make up a few rules to benefit himself. Otherwise, you'll see him buy a house for $50 to put on his Mediterranean Avenue, and then slide it around the corner to his Boardwalk!

16. This is an especially dangerous type of cheat. He's the "selective memory" cheater. When you make a deal with him, he will remember all sorts of conditions later which you never put into the deal. His trick is to include all sorts of possible terms while negotiating and to later pretend that he *thought* you agreed to something which was in fact discussed but dropped from consideration. He will use all sorts of psychological tricks and call all of the other players as witnesses. The only sure way to outfox this guy is to write down all arrangements which have any lasting effect. This may seem like a bother, but it's not half as bad as the screaming which is bound to arise when everyone trusts their memories. If, for some reason, you can't write your deals down, at least repeat

exactly what was agreed on at the conclusion of the negotiations for every trade. Be certain that the other players in the game—the ones who weren't involved in negotiations—hear and understand the arrangements.

17. The last type of cheater is the worst—the liar. Suppose you want to sell him a Red property. You ask him if he has the other two Red properties and he replies, "No, I only have one." So, you sell him your property. Two minutes later, he discovers, "Look at this! I *did* have the other Red property. It was hiding at the bottom of all my money!" It may really have been an accident, but that's no comfort to you. It is illegal to lie to your opponents about which properties you do or do not have. You can mislead your opponents by keeping some properties mortgaged, but you can never lie and tell your opponent that you do not own something which in fact you really do own. The only defense against "accidental discovery" is to know what your opponent does or does not own. Pay attention when properties are bought. Otherwise you become easy prey for the pathological liar.

This concludes the section on some of the more popular forms of cheating. There is one more thing that should be discussed, however. Now that you know how to spot and stop 17 possible ways of cheating, don't rush out and accuse everyone in sight of being a cheater. A lot of honest mistakes happen accidentally in a Monopoly game. Be sure that a player is really cheating *before* you make any accusations, and even then, approach the subject cautiously. Very few people react kindly to being accused of cheating, and the guiltier they are, the louder they'll deny it. In the interest of harmony, find a subtle way to let the cheat know that you are aware of his activities. That should be sufficient to make him stop, at least for the rest of that game.

There is an exception. Sometimes a game of golf with

your boss shows that he has a tendency to add poorly. Likewise, a Monopoly game with the boss can sometimes show that he doesn't count change so well. Don't worry. Worse things could happen.

CHAPTER 17 SUMMARY

    I. Cheater!
   II. The triple Go collector.
  III. Lump sum shortchanging.
  IV. The shifty Banker.
   V. Wrong change maneuvers.
  VI. The Monopoly counterfeiter.
 VII. The quick mover.
VIII. Shake those dice.
  IX. "It's leaning!"
   X. Card cheaters:
      A. Misreaders.
      B. Markers.
      C. Stackers.
      D. Holdouts.
  XI. Title deed mistakes.
 XII. Life sentences.
XIII. Rule creators.
XIV. Selective memory artists.
 XV. The liar.
XVI. Mistakes vs. cheats—use discretion.

Tables

The following tables were taken from the results of the Monopoly Information & Data Analysis System (MIDAS) program, run by the authors at Cornell University in Ithaca, N.Y., on an IBM 370/168 computer, using a PL/C compiler. The initial landing probabilities were computed from a modification of a Markov process, using a 43-state transition matrix. All probabilities given in the tables were rounded to three significant digits, and all dollar amounts and numbers of turns were rounded to the nearest integer.

Both tables show the probabilities of landing on each square on the Monopoly board on any given roll of the dice. Table 1 is organized by color group for easy reference. Table 2 is arranged in order of frequency of landing, from the most frequently visited square (Jail) to the least frequently visited (Mediterranean Avenue).

To interpret the numbers in the tables, ignore the decimal point and you will obtain the average number of times the square in question will be landed on in 10,000 rolls of the dice. In most cases, you will be interested only in the first two significant digits of the probability. These will give you the average number of times the square will be landed on in 1000 rolls. For instance, the line "Atlantic Avenue . . . .0296" means that Atlantic Avenue will be visited an average of 30 times out of every 1000 rolls, or about once in every 34 rolls.

TABLE 1

LANDING PROBABILITIES AND RANKINGS

GROUP	INDIV. PROB.	TOTAL PROB.	RANK*
Purples		.0473	8
Mediterranean Avenue	.0235		
Baltic Avenue	.0238		
Light Blues		.0758	6
Oriental Avenue	.0249		
Vermont Avenue	.0255		
Connecticut Avenue	.0253		
Maroons		.0835	5
St. Charles Place	.0299		
States Avenue	.0254		
Virginia Avenue	.0283		
Oranges		.0969	1
St. James Place	.0312		
Tennessee Avenue	.0329		
New York Avenue	.0328		
Reds		.0953	2
Kentucky Avenue	.0305		
Indiana Avenue	.0299		
Illinois Avenue	.0349		
Yellows		.0874	3
Atlantic Avenue	.0296		
Ventnor Avenue	.0294		
Marvin Gardens	.0284		
Greens		.0858	4
Pacific Avenue	.0294		
No. Carolina Avenue	.0289		
Pennsylvania Avenue	.0275		

* Rank indicates the order of total landing probabilities for color groups

GROUP	INDIV. PROB.	TOTAL PROB.	RANK*
Dark Blues		.0531	7
Park Place	.0241		
Boardwalk	.0290		
Railroads		.1239	
Reading Railroad	.0327		
Pennsylvania Railroad	.0307		
B & O Railroad	.0337		
Short Line Railroad	.0267		
Utilities		.0614	
Electric Company	.0305		
Water Works	.0309		
Chance		.0833	
Square 7	.0254		
Square 22	.0325		
Square 36	.0254		
Community Chest		.0840	
Square 2	.0237		
Square 17	.0306		
Square 33	.0297		
Miscellaneous			
Go	.0340		
Income Tax	.0256		
Just Visiting	.0250		
Jail			
Sent to Jail	.0432		
Spent 1 turn	.0360		
Spent 2 turns	.0300		
Free Parking	.0329		
Go to Jail Square	.0290		
Luxury Tax	.0240		

TABLE 2
LANDING PROBABILITIES BY RANK

RANK	SQUARES	INDIV. PROB.
1	Jail—Sent	.0432
	Spent 1 turn	.0360
	Spent 2 turns	.0300
2	Illinois Avenue	.0349
3	Go	.0340
4	B & O Railroad	.0337
5	Free Parking	.0329
6	Tennessee Avenue	.0329
7	New York Avenue	.0328
8	Reading Railroad	.0327
9	Chance (22)	.0325
10	St. James Place	.0312
11	Water Works	.0309
12	Pennsylvania Railroad	.0307
13	Community Chest (17)	.0306
14	Electric Company	.0305
15	Kentucky Avenue	.0305
16	Indiana Avenue	.0299
17	St. Charles Place	.0299
18	Community Chest (33)	.0297
19	Atlantic Avenue	.0296
20	Pacific Avenue	.0294
21	Ventnor Avenue	.0294
22	Boardwalk	.0290
23	Go to Jail Square	.0290
24	No. Carolina Avenue	.0289
25	Marvin Gardens	.0284
26	Virginia Avenue	.0283
27	Pennsylvania Avenue	.0275
28	Short Line Railroad	.0267
29	Income Tax	.0256
30	Vermont Avenue	.0255

RANK	SQUARES	INDIV. PROB.
31	Chance (36)	.0254
32	Chance (7)	.0254
33	States Avenue	.0254
34	Connecticut Avenue	.0253
35	Just Visiting	.0250
36	Oriental Avenue	.0249
37	Park Place	0241
38	Luxury Tax	.0240
39	Baltic Avenue	.0238
40	Community Chest (2)	.0237
41	Mediterranean Avenue	.0235

TABLE 3

NUMBER OF TURNS TO BREAK EVEN ON YOUR INVESTMENT

Invest-ment	Purple	Lt-Blue	Ma-roon	Orange	Red	Yel-low	Green	Dk-Blue
ZERO	797	490	306	250	240	233	202	175
100	179	72	73	49	—	—	—	—
200	119	63	77	53	60	54	59	47
300	60	54	84	54	63	56	59	47
400	45	31	63	44	63	56	63	.50
500	39	26	57	40	64	57	63	50
600		25	56	38	50	45	65	36
700		23	39	28	50	45	65	36
800		23	32	24	47	41	50	34
900			29	21	45	38	50	34
1000			28	21	45	38	46	25
1100			28	21	34	30	46	25
1200			28	21	28	26	43	23
1300			27	21	28	26	43	23
1400			28	21	25	24	35	24
1500			28	21	26	25	35	24
1600					26	25	31	25
1700					26	26	31	25
1800					29	26	29	26
1900					29	26	29	26
2000					30	27	30	27
2100					28	27	30	
2200					28	27	31	
2300					28	28	31	
2400							31	
2500							31	
2600							32	
2700							32	

Invest-ment	Purple	Lt-Blue	Ma-roon	Orange	Red	Yel-low	Green	Dk-Blue
2800							33	
2900							33	
3000							34	

NOTE: cost of buying properties is only included when fig-uring the number of turns with zero investment.

TABLE 4

EXPECTED CASH OUTPUT PER ROLL
(IN DOLLARS)

Investment	Purple	Lt-Blue	Maroon	Orange	Red	Yellow	Green	Dk-Blue
100	1	2	2	3	—	—	—	—
200	2	3	3	4	4	4	4	7
300	4	6	4	6	6	6	4	7
400	9	8	7	10	6	6	7	9
500	13	13	9	13	7	8	7	9
600		23	11	16	12	14	10	17
700		31	18	26	12	14	10	17
800		34	25	35	17	19	17	24
900			32	44	21	24	17	24
1000			36	49	21	24	23	42
1100			40	54	32	36	23	42
1200			44	59	42	47	29	55
1300			49	64	42	47	29	55
1400			51	69	55	58	41	61
1500			54	74	59	62	41	61
1600					59	62	53	65
1700					63	66	53	65
1800					68	70	64	72
1900					68	70	64	72
2000					72	74	69	76
2100					77	78	69	
2200					77	78	73	
2300					81	82	73	
2400							78	
2500							78	
2600							82	
2700							82	
2800							87	
2900							87	
3000							90	

The effect of Go is to add \$33/turn after taxes.

NOTES ON TABLES 3 AND 4

Tables 3 and 4 are analysis charts. Table 3 measures each color group's efficiency at 30 different levels of investment ($100 increments). The numbers represent how many rolls of the dice it will take you to get your invested money returned at each level of investment. The faster your money is returned, the more *efficient* the color group is at turning your investment into profits. If you have $900 to invest, the chart shows that you can get your money back fastest if you invest it in the Oranges (21 turns). If you scan the chart, you will see that the Oranges are, in general, the most efficient color group. If you have $900 to invest and you don't own the Oranges, the second fastest way to get your money back would be to invest $750 in the Light Blues. (The Light Blues do not have a value on the chart for $900, since the maximum investment you can make in buildings is $750. At $750, it will take you about 23 turns to get your money back.) The formula which was used to compute Table 3 is:

$$\text{Number of rolls} = \frac{\text{u.c.} \times \text{B}}{\sum\limits_{i=1}^{N} P_i R_i}$$

where u.c. = unit development cost (per house)
      B = number of houses to be built
      N = number of properties in the color group
      P_i = probability of landing on property "i"
      R_i = rent on property "i"

Note: when it is possible to arrange houses in more than one way on a color group, the number given in the table is computed assuming the *most efficient* arrangement.

Table 4 (which is used comprehensively in the cash flow section of the Appendix) is a much more useful gauge of a color group's value. Whereas Table 3 tells how efficient a color group is, Table 4 translates that efficiency into the number of dollars you can expect to receive each time the dice are rolled by an opponent who is not immune on your color group. The highest number in each row is enclosed in a box to show which color group returns the most money per turn at each level of investment. If you are investing $900, this table clearly shows that the Oranges are your best investment. On the average, this color group will return you $44 per turn. Why are the Oranges so valuable at this level of investment? Because $900 will develop the Oranges to the critical level, and the critical level is highly profitable.

Your Horoscope

CAPRICORN (The Goat). Dec. 22–Jan. 20.

This is the sign of the cautious Monopoly player. You make trades only when they "feel right," being careful not to be fooled. You are often the underdog, but this does not make you uncomfortable, since you are confident that patience and planning will bring you victory.

Your best token: the shoe. Your best day to play Monopoly: Saturday.

AQUARIUS (The Water Carrier). Jan. 21–Feb. 18.

Your fair mind and cool head make you a respected player in any Monopoly game. To you, the rules are flexible, and you have the ability to display your inventiveness in imaginative trades. You are not afraid to take risks, although you do not play foolishly. Every now and then you make little mistakes that hurt your play.

Your best token: the thimble. Your best day to play Monopoly: Monday.

PISCES (The Fish). Feb. 19–Mar. 20.

Your ability to perceive your opponent's true desires makes you a good player. Your ability to sway people gives you a strong influence over the game, even though at times you prefer to remain silent. Guard against your lack of confidence and use your game-winning abilities. Boardwalk and Park Place seem especially strong for you.

Your best token: the flat iron. Your best day to play Monopoly: Friday.

* * *

ARIES (The Ram). Mar. 21–Apr. 20.

You are the give-'em-hell type and take a back seat to nobody during a Monopoly game. Your imagination and energy will sometimes make you quick-tempered and impatient and will make you appear scornful of other players' advice at times. You spend more time in Jail and roll more doubles than does the average player. Watch out for the Red group.

Your best token: one of your own. Your best day to play Monopoly: Saturday.

TAURUS (The Bull). Apr. 21–May 21.

You are very practical, conservative, and persistent. When you desire a property, you are usually stubborn enough to end up getting it. Those lucky breaks which seem to come your way so often are not all by accident. You like to develop properties slowly, and this can be a strategic error. Chance cards are especially unlucky. Do your best to avoid Pennsylvania Avenue.

Your best token: the dog. Your best day to play Monopoly: Saturday.

GEMINI (The Twins). May 22–June 21.

You are difficult to bankrupt, since your friends always want to give you another chance. You have an excellent wit and should not be afraid to use that wit over the Monopoly board. You get off to slow starts, but come on strong in a long game. Never buy utilities.

Your best token: a $20 double eagle. Best day to play Monopoly: Sunday.

CANCER (The Crab). June 22–July 22.

You derive special joy from bankrupting close friends and relatives, although you try to hide this pride. You are a shrewd investor and don't play hunches. Fight your tendency toward procrastination, which can cause you to pass up golden opportunities. Never forget to roll again on doubles. Beware of Greeks bearing properties.

Your best token: the horseman. Your best Monopoly position: sit on the side of the cheap streets.

LEO (The Lion). July 23–Aug. 23.

This is an excellent sign for a Monopoly player. You are filled with spirit and determination. You will often be impulsive, but not without cause. Watch out for Park Place, as it can knock you out fast. Use your skills to compensate for your frequent streaks of bad luck. Don't fall in love with the player that uses the dog token.

Your best token: the wheelbarrow. Best day to play Monopoly: Thursday.

VIRGO (The Virgin). Aug. 24–Sept. 23.

This is the sign of the analytical mind. Your obsession with details will sometimes get in the way of your trading. Try to relax more during Monopoly games, and your play will improve. Your dislike for screamers is well founded. Do not make partnerships with Leos, as this can upset the stars.

Your best token: the racecar. Your best starting position: second roller.

LIBRA (The Balance). Sept. 24–Oct. 23.

As your symbol implies, you are very good at playing your opponents off against one another. Hotels are very unlucky for you—stick with four houses on each property. Shake the dice well and avoid Luxury Tax. Always cut the Chance cards at the start of the game. Do not become overly concerned if you fall behind early, just don't fall too far behind.

Your best token: the steamboat. Your best day to play Monopoly: Monday.

SCORPIO (The Scorpion). Oct. 24–Nov. 22.

This is the sign of some of the world's best and worst Monopoly players. Be watchful of the housing supply and try not to triple-outguess your opponents. Beware of the trend of almost achieving victory and blowing it at the last moment. Avoid the Income Tax square, as this kind of tax can be the worst.

Your best token: a miniature razor. Your best day to play Monopoly: any day but Saturday.

SAGITTARIUS (The Archer). Nov. 23–Dec. 21.

Your optimistic approach means that you start every game with high hopes. Don't let bad luck discourage you. Don't forget to collect rents, but be careful not to collect rents on Baltic Avenue if it has no houses. Success is yours if you keep your mind from wandering during the game. The Light Blues are a favorable color group.

Your best token: the hat. Your best days to play Monopoly: Wednesdays and holidays.

APPENDIX C

Tips for Games with Other Than Four Players

Two Players

Monopoly games involve a lot more luck and a lot less skill when only two people play. Devices such as partnerships and revenue sharing have no application whatsoever, and giving immunity is equivalent to throwing the properties away. The winner in a two-player game is usually the player who is the first to develop a color group to the critical level. Options are still used in two-player games, and they have the effect of guaranteeing that the player who receives the option will eventually get the optioned property. After all, either he gets it or his opponent does. The only real question is when. Housing shortages are a lot less frequent in two-player games because the players rarely manage to accumulate enough money to buy 32 houses. With four players there is a lot more money at the beginning of the game, and there are more people passing Go and collecting $200. If at all possible, try to get a free land on your opponent's color group. Then, using the free land as a margin of safety, invest all of your available cash, and any other money you can raise, in houses or hotels on your color group. Your hope is to quickly bankrupt your single opponent and win the game. Remember, with only two players in the game, if one gets in trouble there is nobody else around to help bail him out. Go after bankruptcy as quickly as possible, since one unlucky break can undo a lot of skillful playing when only two players are involved.

* * *

Three Players

Strategies in a three-player game are altered somewhat from those in a four-player game. Immunities and partnerships can be used, but their use is extremely limited. In this type of game, it is important to prevent your opponents from trading with one another. The best strategy is to join with another player and gang up on a third player, making sure that you are the one who will do the actual bankrupting and receive the properties. In a three-player game, it is also important to try and bankrupt earlier than in a four-player game, since it is much more difficult to recoup after a bad start. There is still some room to appeal to the third player if you get yourself in rent trouble, but not much. Once again, the dice play a much more important role (or is it roll?) in a three-player game than in a four-player game. In other words, play as skillfully as possible, and be doubly careful to avoid making mistakes. You have much less chance to recover.

Five Players

A Monopoly game gets rather awkward with more than four players (for one thing, there are only four sides to the board), but every now and then you'll find yourself in a five-player game. In a five-player game, the importance of going first or second is increased. Going last in a five-player game can be deadly, so do all you can to buy the right to go first or second if luck doesn't go your way. Owning property, any property, is important in a five-player game. There will always be a lot of trading, so the more properties that you own at the start, the better your chances. If the game lasts awhile and a lot of color groups are developed, be prepared for an early housing shortage. For this reason, the more expensive color groups are a very big risk if it is uncertain that there will be enough time to adequately develop them. Immunities and partnerships can be great in a five-player game. Options, of course, are a lot less valuable, since there are more players to land on an optioned property.

Drawn Games

Although it happens very rarely, it is possible to have a tie game. Assuming that all players have enough cash on hand to survive a run of bad luck, any of the following three positions is a drawn game:

1. All remaining players own color groups which give approximately equal average returns per roll of the dice, and there are no more ways to build houses, which would change those values.

2. One player is receiving more money than the remaining players, but the inflation from the Go salary is enough to give all players positive cash flows. In other words, one player may be getting rich faster than the other players, but no player is getting poorer.

3. There are two players remaining in the game, and each is immune on the other's complete color groups.

But after all, the object of the game isn't to win, it's to have fun!

BESTSELLERS FROM DELL

fiction

- [ ] ERIC by Doris Lund............................. $1.75 (4586-04)
- [ ] MARATHON MAN by William Goldman.......... $1.95 (5502-02)
- [ ] WINTER KILLS by Richard Coneon............... $1.75 (6007-00)
- [ ] THE OTHER SIDE OF MIDNIGHT by Sidney Sheldon $1.75 (6067-07)
- [ ] THE RHINEMANN EXCHANGE by Robert Ludlum.. $1.95 (5079-13)
- [ ] THE LONG DARK NIGHT by Joseph Hayes....... $1.95 (4824-06)
- [ ] SHAMPOO by Robert Alley..................... $1.75 (7808-17)
- [ ] PLEASURE MAN by Mae West.................. $1.50 (7074-06)
- [ ] THE NAKED FACE by Sidney Sheldon............. $1.25 (4921-05)
- [ ] DOG DAY AFTERNOON by Patrick Mann......... $1.50 (4519-06)
- [ ] THE BOY WHO INVENTED THE BUBBLE GUN
  by Paul Gallico $1.50 (0719-28)

nonfiction

- [ ] JAMES DEAN, THE MUTANT KING by David Dalton $1.75 (4893-02)
- [ ] MIKE ROY'S CROCK COOKERY................. $1.25 (5617-04)
- [ ] THE FEMALE WOMAN by Anianna Stassinopoulous. $1.50 (5015-02)
- [ ] MAN KIND? by Cleveland Amory................ $1.75 (5451-03)
- [ ] CHARLES BRONSON SUPERSTAR by Steven Whitney $1.50 (4561-11)
- [ ] THE JAWS LOG by Carl Gottlieb................. $1.50 (4689-00)
- [ ] THE REICH MARSHAL by Leonard Mosley........ $1.75 (7686-06)
- [ ] JOEY by Donald Goddard...................... $1.75 (4825-05)
- [ ] DR. STILLMAN'S 14-DAY SHAPE-UP PROGRAM
  by I. M. Stillman, M.D., and S. S. Baker.......... $1.75 (1913-04)
- [ ] WHY MEN CALL GIRLS by Shannon Canfield
  and Dick Stuart $1.50 (9609-06)

Buy them at your local bookstore or send this page to the address below:

DELL BOOKS
P.O. BOX 1000, PINEBROOK, N.J. 07058

Please send me the books I have checked above. I am enclosing $_____
(please add 25¢ per copy to cover postage and handling). Send check or
money order—no cash or C.O.D.'s.

Mr/Mrs/Miss_____

Address_____

City_____State/Zip_____

This offer expires 11/76